PLATINUM
ENTREPRENEUR

"If you can dream it, you can do it."
Walt Disney

Photo taken by: Nancy Le

PLATINUM ENTREPRENEUR

A GEN-Z ENTREPRENEUR'S GUIDE TO ESTABLISHING AN EMPIRE

Jacob M. Melendez

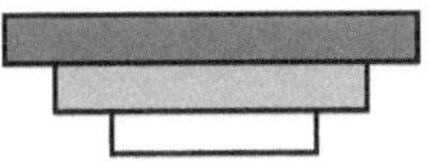

E X C I T E PUBLISHING

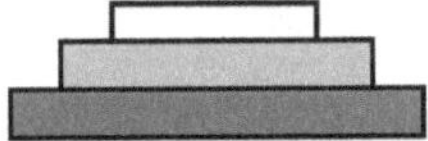

A subsidiary of **E L E V A T E**

"I came in to win, you know. This is why I stay up late while other people are sleeping."

Sean "Diddy" Combs

To my mother who has loved and supported me every step of the way…

TABLE OF CONTENTS

INTRODUCTION

Individual expression, business and the idea of being confident enough in yourself to actually chase your dreams in real-time is what gives me a rush to wake up every day. I did not know that I was actually creative to any extent, and it was because I had never pursued exactly what Jacob desired. For me, I always wanted to experience massive success, but I was torn between completely creating my own world and pursuing what I loved, or satisfying the rest of the world by always staying quiet and playing my part in the system. I knew that what made me happiest was being able to be my complete self, which is a very creative, ambitious, competitive, energetic and happy soul. It is because of this that I chose to pursue entrepreneurship.

I have always been an overachiever, but I have not always been confident in myself. From childhood I was always wanting to be something not just bigger than myself, but absolutely massive. I thought it was going to be through football, but after tearing my ACL during my freshman year of high school, I quickly realized that I did not want to put my body on the line anymore. It was at that point that I took my dedicated, competitive and overachieving mindset to the field of business. I quickly realized that this is where I belonged because it was in this field that I found myself finally coming in first on a consistent basis, and as a natural competitor, that is exactly what you want.

Through personal experience, I have found that entrepreneurship is all about consistency and self-belief. I always had the first, but not the latter, and that is what held me back for a long time from becoming who I truly wanted to be. I always knew what I wanted to do, but I was too afraid to pursue that path. I have learned that no one knows everything, and you will always have naysayers. Anytime I feel afraid to do something, I tell myself, "Life is too short, and you only get one in human history. Do what you want." I had a large extent of social anxiety growing up, but as I started paying attention to those around me, I realized that many others did as well. It understanding this and becoming angry at my own insecurities that helped me find the confidence in myself to finally pursue what I wanted.

Nowadays, I will gladly tell you that I do wake up at 3:40am in order get started working on my businesses; Elevate and Excite Publishing (Elevate Subsidiary). I also have a huge passion for stock investing/trading, and every single day I wake up, I get to do exactly that. All of this could have went a completely opposite way for me on many occasions, but because I stayed consistent and found empowerment in my uniqueness, life is what I wanted it to be.

My mission in writing this book is to empower you by guiding you on how to establish a business that is relative to Generation Z. I believe that every ambitious and innovative young soul needs access to as many resources as possible, and that is exactly what this book aims to achieve. Entrepreneurship can be rough, and oftentimes you have to learn to pick yourself up off the ground. Nevertheless, I am here to not only educate you but to truly make you realize that you can literally do anything that you want if you get realistic about it and become self-aware.

Entrepreneurship is not for the weak-minded but for the mind that has been told he/she cannot do something or was not good enough on countless occasions. It is a journey for the ones who are truly self-motivated and confident in their ideas. True players and game changers are ones who are able to look at their inner being and realize what exactly they must do in order to make their dreams become a reality, and this book will provide insight into how exactly you can do that for yourself.

Enjoy.

— Jacob M. Melendez

CHAPTER ONE:

WHAT IS AN ENTREPRENEUR?

CHAPTER ONE

In order to fully understand entrepreneurship, we must be able to define what an entrepreneur is and the mindset behind one. Maybe you have a goal of becoming a musician, singer, rap artist, painter, writer, business owner, etc. If this is you, it is possible that you have entrepreneurial aspirations. Any of these occupations listed requires an individual to use his/her own creativity and initiative in order to make money.

Simply put, an entrepreneur is someone who has an idea and is able to sell it for revenue. Obviously, there is much more to an entrepreneur, but in the grand scheme of one's pursuit, an entrepreneur is ultimately trying to produce a stream of revenue with his/her idea whether it be a for-profit or non-profit business. Some notable entrepreneurs are Mark Zuckerberg, Kanye West, Jay-Z, Sean "Diddy" Combs, Oprah Winfrey, Ellen DeGeneres, and Ariana Grande. Each of these individuals are widely known for having success in selling their own products/services.

Often times when we are beginning our entrepreneurial journey, it can be easy to think that someone in corporate America with a suit is an entrepreneur. However, this is not the case, but because entrepreneurship is directly related to business, it can be easy to think this way. Remember that an entrepreneur is a businessman, but a businessman is not necessarily an entrepreneur. One is a business founder and the other is an employee of a business that was founded by someone else (the entrepreneur). That is not to say that an employee cannot develop a profitable idea for his/her employer and become an entrepreneur as well. However, the type of entrepreneurship we will be discussing in this book is that of someone creating his/her own business.

To be considered an entrepreneur, you must have the ability to transform your thoughts into dollars. There are some individuals who have stellar ideas, but they end up falling short of making these become a reality because they do not know how to turn it into a paycheck and neither does anyone associated with them. Turning dreams to dollars is a process that has no blueprint, and as an entrepreneur, a recurring challenge is to be constantly thinking of how to profitably implement your ideas. There is no timestamp or promotions, and no one can tell you exactly what to do in order to have success because at the end of the day, it is your own unique vision, and it is up to you to make money.

One key trait of an entrepreneur is that he/she is a risk taker. This is not to say that one should jump off of a cliff because he/she was told to so, but instead an entrepreneur should take calculated risks. Every decision from hiring members to posting content can pose a risk to an entrepreneur, so it is important that this person properly manages the risk/reward of each investment. While an entrepreneur must be cautious when taking risks, this individual is not one who is timid in any sense to pull the trigger when he/she sees a reasonable opportunity to be pursued. Without risk, there would be no Apple, Google, TD Ameritrade, etc. These were all businesses that started within the minds of individuals who were calculated risk takers.

Conversely, while it might seem as though many entrepreneurs follow their dreams, there is also a great number who instead represent opportunists. Rather than executing and perfecting a certain passion within a specific industry, some entrepreneurs seek out profitable opportunities within an already developed market. For instance, a hot topic of discussion the past few years has been the marijuana industry. If an entrepreneur was not necessarily passionate about the plant but realized that by creating a business that dealt with medical marijuana, profits could be produced, he/she might be willing to invest capital into this idea.

Nevertheless, there is no right or wrong approach to entrepreneurship. Simply put, there is only success and failure, and you either succeed at integrating your ideas in a profitable manner or you fail. To be an entrepreneur, you might find that it requires a certain level of obsession in order to truly master your craft and become a titan at running your business. Whether you are a dream fulfiller or opportunist, the success of your entrepreneurial journey "is just actions away."

CHAPTER TWO:

TARGET AUDIENCE

CHAPTER TWO

As aspiring entrepreneurs, we often pursue our ideas with a big picture mindset, and while it is beneficial to know your end goal, you cannot reach that point if you do not know who is buying your products/services. The topic of choosing a target audience is often discussed, but it is not emphasized to the extent that it should be, and failure to identify this can serve as a major obstacle that will prevent you from meeting your objectives.

Let us say that you are a clothing designer who is the best of the best when it comes to developing unique and intriguing designs. Nevertheless, your problem is that you are investing all your time into designing and marketing, but you are getting nothing in return. You wonder what the problem is and why people are not purchasing your products. It is hard for you to identify the issue because you have friends who are telling you that your clothing designs are exceptional. While this may be true, you are not selling because you have not been able to pinpoint your target audience. However, your competition is on fire with sales because they have taken the time to sit down and identify the demographics that align with the character of their brand.

In going the extra mile to understand what their brand stands for and what products they sell, your competition has been able to identify their target audience. In order to successfully create a loyal customer base, you must craft your brand and business in a way that aligns with the preferences of your target audience. Without defining these boundaries, it is near impossible to have a profitable business. Realize and accept that you cannot sell to everyone due to multiple factors and get serious about defining your target audience.

What Separates You?

Discovering your target audience can be difficult, especially when you are just starting to pursue your business ideas because believe it or not, you may not even know what your business is selling. You know that your business is a clothing company, but you must also be able to identify what truly separates it from the plethora of other clothing companies. If you are a sportswear brand, what makes you stand out from Nike, Adidas and Under Armour? You cannot just pose as a mere sportswear company who mimics the designs of your competitors.

You must find the unique niche that your brand represents. For example, instead of just targeting athletes and individuals who follow name brand sportswear, maybe you should target track runners who are in high school and are not able to reach first place. You must identify the issue that your product/service can solve and look at similar businesses to decide what it is that you can offer to separate yourself from them.

Nevertheless, while you might find a unique idea that separates you from others in your industry, you need to recognize if this idea is truly making an impact on others in a manner that keeps them wanting more. If people admire the products/services and uniqueness your business has to offer, they will continue to follow because they will want to know what is next. Uniqueness is genius.

After successful singers and musicians release music, their fans are always excited about what the outcome of the sound will be for their next album or song. Thousands of fans each day are scrolling through various social media platforms to view their favorite artists' music videos, interviews and other updates. This happens because while there is a seemingly endless number of musical artists in the world, the ones who are truly successful are able to inspirationally distinguish themselves from others in their industry. It is important to notice why it is that you connect with a certain artist or celebrity more deeply than maybe some of your peers might. Understanding this will show you that the branding of that person aligns with your character in a certain way.

Why Are You Selling?

Finding a target audience can seem like a simple and common-sense task, but it is very easy to overlook this aspect when you and those around you are caught up in the excitement about the potential your business idea holds. You must ask yourself who exactly you are selling to, but you must also ask the question of why you are selling your desired product/service. If it is a for-profit, obviously you are selling to make money, but what is the deeper meaning?

Maybe you are trying to help others become more knowledgeable about certain software tools or inspire someone to use methods to improve their social media traffic. These are examples of great goals, but what is the result you want to see from achieving them? Possibly, from the software tools business, you might want to see clients become more efficient with their own business ideas as a result of your training course. For the social media course, you would probably want to see the client gain a large and interactive following of loyal customers as a result of your training services. It is important to know why you are selling a product/service to a target audience because this lets you know if you are satisfying your following and reaching your goals.

How Will You Sell?

Moreover, once you have taken the time to identify your target audience, what you are selling and why you are selling, you must then determine how you will go about distributing your brand and business to the public. It is easy to believe that brand and business have the same meaning because they are often used in place of one another, but you must realize that your brand is the identity and perception of your business. The business itself however, is made up of the physical actions taken in order to produce revenue. Apple for example, is a business that sells smartphones, smartwatches, tablets and computers. Their brand however, is the respected, creative, classy and inspirational perception they produce.

Often times, people like to buy the brand more than the actual business. As an entrepreneur, you have to decide what business you are in. Yes, you may sell clothes, but what business are you really in? Maybe you are actually in the photo business because that is the medium through which you create exposure for your clothes. When you are deciding how you will go about getting your products/services recognized, it is important to keep your target audience in mind because knowing what is influential to them will help bring the most traffic to your business.

Get creative about your methods of selling your brand and business. If you are a clothing company, then maybe instead of hosting a sale, you could surprise your subscribers and send them a bracelet or shirt in the mail. The more genuinely unique you can be, the more likely you are to have success when it comes to defining the boundaries for your target audience. If you are able to creatively and successfully execute a means of distributing your products and services, your audience will appreciate the fact that they chose you instead of someone else.

Be Transparent (You)

As young entrepreneurs, some of us dream about wanting to serve as an influence to other people. If this is the case, you will want to be as transparent as possible about who you are. One key way to reveal this is by posting videos and pictures to social media. No one can be influenced by you if they do not know who you are, so that is why you must show your face. People love to have someone to watch and look up to, and if you can become that influence for your target audience, you will be more likely to succeed. This is why influence is more important than revenue. People buy the influence that comes from your uniqueness, and if you can deliver it to them properly, this will give you an edge over your competition.

However, you do need to be careful because often times, as young entrepreneurs, it is easy to get into that competitive mind state. Ego is often connected with this, and if that is how you are feeling when talking, you do not need to direct that energy towards anyone. It is very important to stay humble when representing yourself because an arrogant portrayal of pride can come off as very unattractive to your audience.

Aside from using videos and photos to influence your following, you can also start a blog that will allow them to get to know you more. You have the power to help people, but you cannot do this unless you are able to be transparent and confident in who you are as a person. The most influential hip hop artists are the ones who can relate to us by revealing their true identities and struggles through their music. Transparency as a person is very important because it opens up the door for you to influence your audience. Influence turns into revenue, and it also gives you longevity because loyal customers will always want more from you and your business if you give them the chance to know and respect you.

Be Transparent (Business)

When you are an entrepreneur, people want to know what it is that you do to make money. Sometimes, it can be obvious, especially if you work from a physical location like a tire shop or appliance store. People see the building and the workers, so it is very transparent. However, if you are an internet entrepreneur and connect through a lot of social media posts, it can be difficult to know what you actually do to make money. There are certain individuals on the internet nowadays who pose as entrepreneurs of very successful businesses, but in reality, their business is YouTube. They need your views, so what they do is sell you all of this advice and information to pose as someone credible, but without you subscribing and listening to them, they probably would not be successful. However, as a young entrepreneur, it is important to be as transparent as possible because you do not have the benefit of age in this case, which would allow you to seem as though you had a great amount of experience and success.

Merely posting on the internet as a 19-year-old giving advice can sometimes look like that is all you have to offer because at 19, how much success can you really have? It is very possible and realistic that you have had great success, but if this is the case, you need to be very transparent about it and help others see what exactly it is that your business does to produce revenue. You can do this by providing in depth discussions, or you can even show people the different processes that go on behind the scenes of your business.

Both of these are great for providing transparency to your audience, and always keep in mind that the more you reveal, the better and more credible you will become. If you can establish an influence as an entrepreneur and a business, you will have a more realistic chance at gaining traction in your industry.

Consistency

When tending to your target audience and establishing influence upon them, you must stay consistent with your values and principles but also with your dedication to your work. Getting established can be a difficult and exhausting hustle, so it is important that you do not lack in consistency until you have comfortably been able to pay your bills and employ others with your business. This could take years to accomplish, but if you start to give in and get lazy with satisfying your target audience, you will lose the power to influence them. Instead of elevating your character into a more credible and popular category, you will only end up falling back down to level one. If you want to continue climbing the ladder of gradual growth, you must remain consistent.

When developing your brand, you need to know the values and principles that it stands for because this will help you identify your target audience. Once you identify them, you need to stay consistent with these values and principles because switching, especially in the beginning, can serve as a detriment to your growth. You have already established an audience that you want to impact, so changing up what you stand for could confuse them and cause them to stop following you because you have gotten rid of what makes you special.

Moreover, it is equally as important to stay consistent with your business actions because if you just decide that you do not feel like doing something one day, you will suffer the consequences. As stated earlier, the game of entrepreneurship is not sympathetic to you in any way. If you want to be able to influence and expand your target audience, your work ethic has to stay consistent, and you must continue to conquer each level of success.

Entrepreneurial success that is built to last takes a great amount of patience and relentless commitment to your business. You cannot afford to half way commit to your job at the beginning if you truly want to thrive and eventually employee others. Your target audience needs to be your main focus as an entrepreneur, and if you cannot learn to put them first, you will not be able to manifest success because you will not act in a manner that shows you value them. Show consistency in your commitment to your brand and business every single day because this will allow your influence on your target audience to grow stronger.

Focus on Pleasing Your Target Audience

Knowing who you are and what you stand for is very important when you are an entrepreneur because you will find that it is impossible to please everyone. However, you must understand that this is because not everyone's characteristics will fit within the scope of your target audience. You will have many elders and peers who do not agree with your ideas or see your vision, but part of being an entrepreneur is having the confidence to attempt transforming your uniqueness into profits.

It is not always easy to understand someone's vision right away. That is why it is crucial for you to carefully focus on expressing your vision to your target audience by the way you choose to market your brand and perform your business obligations. Trying to please everyone at once with your decisions and your values/principles can result in a failure of your business because you will be torn when wondering how to portray yourself.

While being an entrepreneur does have stellar benefits such as reward and recognition, it definitely has its downfalls. One of those downfalls is the fact that some people may start to dislike you or criticize you. It is very easy to feel like you are irritating people or annoying them when you are advertising and marketing for your business.

What you have to understand is that this is part of the life. It is not meant for the lighthearted who are afraid to speak their minds. You have to claim your stake in the game, and to make that happen, you have to push and market your business by discussing your intentions.

Expression cannot be lacked when you are developing and discovering your target audience. The people that do not appreciate you and find you annoying probably did not like you to begin with, so nothing new is really occurring in this case. Also, those who do not personally know you should not even impact the way you choose to carry yourself. It is not good for your growth as a business or person to sacrifice your character and stay quiet in order to please those who do not agree with you. If you have respect and integrity, by all means distribute the message of your brand as much as you possibly can in different ways.

People who criticize you were not meant to be included in your target audience, so you have to be confident in yourself and your vision because you do not want to feel obligated to please them. If you are an entrepreneur, you have to stand up for your idea and be strong, especially if you are young.

Never feel discouraged about your idea or your process around anyone. It does not matter if they have a doctorates degree from Harvard. You cannot lack confidence in yourself because that will give people a chance to tear you and your business down.

Entrepreneurship, while primarily about helping others solve problems, is also about displaying confidence in your ideas and getting people to know that you are serious about your business. If you can stand strong in your decisions and surround yourself with people that care about you, you will find it much easier to not focus on the critics and wise guys. You have to be yourself because that is the unique energy that brings value to your brand. Accept that not everyone is a fan of you and relentlessly apply yourself to truly mold your ideas into a profitable reality.

Focusing on your target audience instead of your critics will allow you to remain in more of a positive mind state. It will also hold you accountable because you will feel the need to help those who admire and respect your ideas. When you are in a positive state of mind, you are more likely to feel comfortable with your uniqueness and creativity, which is exactly the reason your target audience follows you rather than someone else.

The best way to make sure you are focusing on your target audience is by communicating with them as much as you can. Develop and maintain a relationship, so that your following can feel comfortable when they are dealing with your business. This can be anything from music to lawn mowing services. It does not matter what type of business you have. When your following feels comfortable, you will always have a target audience that is satisfied with your products/services and intrigued by the uniqueness your brand portrays. Focus on presenting yourself as an influence to your following, and serve as a benefit to their lives through your words, actions and results.

CHAPTER THREE:

THE POWER OF FREE

CHAPTER THREE

Every entrepreneur's goal is to produce revenue from a product/service that he/she is selling. However, this can be difficult when you are first starting out because most likely, your brand and business do not have a strongly established amount of credibility and/or popularity, especially if you are in your late teens or early 20s. This is why it is necessary to promote your business through free giveaways or heavy incentives. Everyone loves free, and if you are able to provide a quality product or service without charge, you will find it easier to gain exposure and establish a loyal following.

Truly, when you first begin executing your business ideas, you will be experimenting a great amount because you have probably not yet discovered what does and does not work for your business. Do not be discouraged however, as it is impossible to completely know everything your brand stands for when you first begin.

You only see your brand from your perspective, but you do not see it from your clients' perspective, so it is important that you gain as much credibility as you can during this stage. Providing your first wave of followers with incentives and free items will cause them to have more respect for you and your business. Doing this shows that you are not just about making money, but you actually believe that your idea can serve as a benefit to the lives of those you are targeting. You must realize that exceptional entrepreneurship is about ethically satisfying the customer. Promoting your business with free items and incentives will show that you genuinely value your following.

Why in the World Would I Give?

The answer to this question is the simple fact that you are a young and new entrepreneur with almost no credibility or recognition outside of your hometown. You need to understand that an overwhelming majority of the world does not know anything about you or your product.

The only way you are going to get your name discovered is by providing worthy incentives to your stakeholders because this will provide credibility. It will also serve as a tool the will allow you to transform from being an unknown amateur to a recognized and credible professional in your industry. If you can become an influence and grow your following, you can get your hands into just about any industry, and your audience will follow you.

If it was that easy to make money from the beginning, everyone would be an entrepreneur, but the reality is that entrepreneurship is a constant hustle, and getting established can be very challenging and unfulfilling if you do not execute it with the customer first approach. Individuals will see and respect your hustle, and some might even become inspired by it, which will cause them to look forward to purchasing your products as you begin to level up. The goal is to progress towards making your idea your primary source of income in order to pay the bills and enjoy your life. To get to that point, you must respect each level and start from the very first one, which is free but influential.

Mere Selling is a Bad Recipe for Success

It is amazing to put your time and energy towards increasing sales for your business, but if you are on social media and constantly just posting the product in hopes that it will sell, you should probably stop. You are not showing that you value your customers, and you are not giving your brand any depth. This only hurts you because there is no uniqueness being expressed, and it does not look like you have anything that you really stand for. If there is no brand representation when you are marketing your products, you can easily go unnoticed with the rest.

You must place yourself in the shoes of those viewing your products and understand if your marketing is representative of what the brand and business stands for. It is not difficult to ask your followers on social media what they enjoy most about your business. Always focus on the connection between the perception of your brand and target audience when marketing your business. If you are able to display confidence and belief in your brand, your followers will do the same. Just discussing your business services/products is not enough. You must show that you care about your customers and that your brand stands for what they believe in.

You Are Not an Expert

People like to buy from the best of the best, and when you are beginning as a young entrepreneur, you are nowhere near the top of your industry. This is why it is important to express yourself and exercise emphasis on the value of your brand by selling free products/services.

Many music artists begin by uploading their content to free music streaming services, and it benefits them because it allows them to develop their following and establish their brand. While these people are not yet masters of their industry, they are gaining a loyal following and earning respect by providing free labor. This also shows that they are very dedicated and passionate about their ideas, and that produces respect as well.

You must "earn your keep" if you will, in order to establish yourself as a force to be reckoned with in your industry, and the path of free giveaways allows you to move more quickly towards that title. Revenue may not need to be your main focus at the beginning because you could end up burning yourself out and finding that all of your work has led to hardly any sales.

Many people fail in business because they put so much money towards their idea and immediately try to sell products/services to people, but they totally forget about the importance of the brand and establishing their following. Respect the hustle of being young and new to entrepreneurship, and realize that the power of free is a powerful step that will allow you to gradually move from amateur to expert.

More Publicity

Another benefit of selling your products/services for free is the fact that your brand will receive more publicity because it will have the potential to spread more quickly. Indeed, if you have a sportswear business, you might decide that you want to give out bracelets each time someone buys a product from you, or maybe you want to post inspirational videos online. Providing these types of incentives will allow people to get a more in-depth look at your brand, which will result in stronger customer loyalty that may spread by word of mouth. You have to realize that entrepreneurship is a gradual scale, so every time you give a free product, your brand name spreads just a little bit more.

The goal is to be able to establish a loyal following that takes pride in your product. If people have pride, their peers will see that and be influenced to purchase from your business. You can view your free giveaways as a mad scientist would view infecting the population with a lethal virus. It goes from one person to another, then two, three and so on until you experience exponential growth.

While free giveaways do provide your brand the benefit of spreading more quickly, you will need to stay consistent with your plan. For instance, if you like to reward your email subscribers with incentives on certain occasions, you will want to always do this when these times come around. A lack of consistency could result in a reduction of your following and influence. When you are first starting out, the last thing you want is a reduction in your already small following, so make sure that you show your customers you value them through your consistency. Again, if you keep the customers as your number one priority, you will experience gradual success and publicity.

More publicity can be a positive, but it can also be bad for business if you are not staying true to your brand's values and principles. If you are doing free giveaways for inspirational bracelets, do not suddenly come out and start selling depressing or degrading messages. You have already started to establish a loyal following, and if you sell something (even for free) that is contradictory to your original values, you will lose customers and the potential to gain positive publicity. Keep your free giveaways consistent on a timely and principle basis, and you will be able to maintain your following and spread your brand's message.

How to Go About Executing the Power of Free

Depending on the products/services your business provides, the best way to go about exercising the power of free is by using your social media. If you want to go about communicating that you are doing a free giveaway, you can post to apps like Twitter, Instagram, Facebook, Reddit,

Snapchat, etc. If you do this, you will have people who like what they see, and because it is free, they will not mind having one of your products.

You cannot be insecure when you are taking on social media because if you let this anxiety cripple you, you will never grow. People do not want to purchase products from someone who has zero confidence in his/her business, even if it is free. If they do purchase, it is probably because they feel bad for you, but they will most likely not use your product in public. "Using your social media" is a broad term. On these different platforms, you can do things such as post pictures, videos, hashtags, etc. to inspire people to view your website and your products/services. It is all about the customer, and if they want something new every day, then you give them something new every day.

Using your email is another powerful tool for spreading awareness about free products because you are sending messages to followers who are subscribed to your business and excited to see what is next. Your subscribers need to know that they are appreciated and valued, so you should be sending emails to them on a regular basis to discuss deals and information about the business. If you can keep your subscribers satisfied, their loyalty to your brand will continue to grow, and their pride in your products/services will be seen by others around them.

As you progress and become more serious about your business, you will start to use critical thinking skills in order to grow your following by exercising the power of free. You will probably not become rich overnight with your idea, so providing free products/services can only help you extend your influence and increase your client base. Give them free now, and later they will want to pay you.

Platinum Entrepreneur

CHAPTER FOUR:

THE PUSH

CHAPTER FOUR

Everyone sees the shine, but only a few see the grind. We all know that Travis Scott is a successful rap artist, but what really makes him the overarching influence that excites us and has us following every song he drops, every album, music video, etc.? For years, he has been building his influence through various channels and mediums of communication. He did not just wake up, make a few songs for SoundCloud and disappear. In order to build an aura of that caliber, you must apply yourself to the process of developing your brand and business every single day. The push is what takes place behind the scenes, and that in itself is the true business you end up dealing with. You might think that when you go into business as a clothing designer, author or music artist, you will get to sit back and only do that. However, you have to realize that there is so much more work to do in different areas if you want to make a living. You have to be a businessman, and you have to be willing to hustle with your mind, body and spirit. The behind the scenes grind, or the push, is the key to entrepreneurial success.

What is No Push?

In order to understand the concept of the push, you must understand what it means to have no push. Think about it this way: when you were young, you might have been afraid to jump off of the diving board at your local swimming pool. However, your sibling came and pushed you, and after that you were no longer afraid to jump. Entrepreneurship is the same way, except you cannot expect someone to come and make you do your job every day. You must be the push behind your business that moves it to new heights of success. Everyone will see the glamour that rests on the outside, but they will not see you working when you have not even showered yet and are doing the little things for your business such as automating a subscriber message list or editing a video. It is these things that can either trip you up or help you move to the next level of success as an entrepreneur.

It does not matter what industry you are in. If you are not contributing to your idea every single day, you will not experience growth. It is immature to dream so large but yet work so little. That is entitlement, and thinking this way will only lead you to a slow realization that life did not turnout the way you had desired. The last thing any entrepreneur wants is to one day wake up and realize that his/her dreams are not respected and matured enough to become a reality. Being young is very beneficial in many ways because you have energy and ambition. You are also naïve, which means that you do not yet know everything that comes with the business you are in, so you are willing to try more things. Nevertheless, if you never try while you are young and take your dreams seriously, you will not manifest success. Do you want to get paid millions? That is no small amount, and if it was as easy as your mind is subconsciously capable of making it seem, everyone on this planet would be self-employed millionaires.

Being young is difficult because our family or someone close to us pays the bills while we work and go to school, so the concept of reality is not as easy to grasp until we get out into the world and realize that we do not have much of anything. You literally have to build something from the ground up with whatever resources you have.

Entrepreneurship is not a hobby. It is a full time and overtime job. You have to constantly want better for yourself and others. There is zero room for laziness or entitlement, and if you let this continue to dominate your way of thinking, people on the outside will see it and not want anything to do with you because you are not working. What is there to respect about your push if it does not exist? If you have nothing to do on a Sunday, and you are always thinking of becoming a great artist, do not watch Netflix. Work on your art and learn how to start making small dollars for your work. It is a gradual climb of success, and you are going to have to earn every single follower, dollar and compliment you receive.

Entrepreneurship is not for the weak, but only for the willing who are hustlers that want to educate themselves and make the lives of their clients better. You have to stop lying in bed all day and thinking about how your life is going to be so much better because of your idea. You instead need to start thinking about how the life of those who follow and buy your products/services will benefit.

It is not about you. It is about the customer, and if you are doing nothing because you do not feel motivated, you are not caring about your customers or even trying to grow your following. In this case, the chances are that you have no brand developed, no following established besides your close friends and no money made. This in itself is not influential at all, and if you are wondering why you have not experienced success or any type of breakthrough yet, that is your answer. Realize that the entrepreneurs you look up to are able to pay the bills and employ people, but it is because they were also on level one of success and built their brand and business up every single day from that point. You must have a sense of reality in order to develop your ideas into a source of income.

The phrase, "every single day" needs to be emphasized because that is the key to gradual success. If you are applying yourself every single day to the development of your business and brand, you will be more likely to succeed. However, if you are allowing your lack of motivation and laziness to stop you, you are in the wrong business and do not belong in the field of entrepreneurship. This game does not care how young, inexperienced or unfortunate you might be. It does not have sympathy for you, and if you want to really show the world who you are, then you must work every single day to master your craft and push your business into the swimming pool of gradual success.

Different Hats

We all see these huge corporations who have their marketing department, human resources, accounting, etc., but when you are a young and new entrepreneur, you can expect to probably have to learn most of these jobs on your own. You might have a friend or two that is working with you or willing to help, but for the most part, you will have to learn these aspects because it is your business and no one except you has the same amount of ambition to make it grow. If you want it to grow, you must learn the functions of different software, cameras, apps, etc. because these are the tools you will need in order to get your business noticed. If you are willing to take the time to execute all of the tools that you can, establishing your brand and producing results for your business will become much easier.

Patience can be difficult to have in our fast-changing internet world, but if you want to learn different aspects of your business, then you must have the patience to sit back and strengthen weak skillsets. For instance, let us say that that you are an app designer, and you know all there is to making an app as perfect as it needs to be. However, once you encounter the business aspect, you realize that you do not know how to go about marketing your app. You also have subpar social skills, which makes you feel too insecure about posting videos. Despite your excitement to discuss the app with your peers, you need to take a deep breath and learn about marketing and presenting skills. Watch as many necessary videos as you can and take in the information you are given. You can even create a social media account, lock it and make practice posts for your business. Nobody will see it except you and those you approve. While it is important that you become a master of your craft (app designing in this case), you do not have much besides yourself when you are starting, so invest in yourself and learn all aspects of the business.

Focus

The push is something that must be visited every day when you are a young entrepreneur, so it is important that you learn to focus and get away from distracting energy. Sometimes that energy can be you, so you need to make sure that you are able to create as much of a happy but focused environment as possible. That could mean turning the lights off and playing instrumental music, or it could mean opening a window up and working, but regardless you need to know what works for you.

Your environment needs to be one that is motivating as well, because you are more focused when you are motivated. For those who might have ADHD, as stated earlier, you need to find what works best for you. If you cannot do well while sitting down, perhaps find a way to work while pacing or standing up. An entrepreneur does not look for excuses, but he/she instead looks for opportunities. Opportunities come, but if you do not focus enough to prepare yourself for them, they will pass you and visit the next person.

Establishing yourself as an entrepreneur is all about creating as powerful of a foundation as you possibly can. In order to be able to build a strong foundation, you must have the endurance and consistency to be able to focus in every single day and lay down the bricks of your business. This can mean posting daily content to social media, cold calling, selling door to door, etc. To run a business when you are first beginning takes a lot of dedication because if you are young, you most likely do not have access to what would be considered an adequate amount of team members. For this reason, you need to be able to focus on managing various aspects day in and day out in order to make sure that the foundation of your business is as strong as possible.

Does Your Hustle Compete with the Big Leagues?

Your answer to this question will tell you if you are stuck in the high school mentality or if you are truly an entrepreneur trying to create a business. High school is fun because you get to dream and think that everything will go your way eventually. You tell yourself that you will do whatever it takes to make it, and you picture success in your mind. However, you never think about your actual process, and if you do act on a process, it is only when you have the motivation to do so. That is why you must escape this mentality because there is nothing realistic about it.

If you truly want to grow your business and get the shine, you must stop worrying about your insecure peers who talk down to you. Put yourself out there, and ask the question again of, “Would a corporate executive invest in my push?” If the answer is no, then you need to mature your process and your commitment. How do you expect to be a boss one day or even produce a stable means of income for yourself if you are half way committed to your push? The push is everything, and you have to understand that there are 60-year-old executives with all the money in the world who are hiring young people with energy like yourself to work for them and advance their business. Can your dedication and work ethic compete with this? You have to think about how to pay the bills with your idea, and you have to stop thinking about just the big picture.

There is no better time than right now to get started on your hustle. Even if you have no money, it is 2019, and you need to have the grit to make things happen. Entrepreneurs make their ideas happen for them in a profitable manner. If you want something bad enough, you need to get serious and meet up with professionals in the industry.

Communicate your thoughts and ideas with them and get a taste of what their process is like as well. Doing this will not only give you more knowledge about how they operate, but it will also bring confidence to you. Once you talk to true businessmen and see that they are people just like you, you will be able to pursue your ideas with genuine confidence and start to take the development of your brand and business more seriously. To become the best, you must know how the best operate, and understand that they are far more equipped than you when you are first beginning. This is why you must have a push behind the scenes and learn to invest your efforts into all aspects of your business that are necessary in order for you to increase value.

Loneliness

Entrepreneurship is a lonely path at times, so it is important that you realize this before you decide to push your business forward. It is a long ride, and if you cannot accept the fact that you will probably spend a lot of time alone, you will not have an effective push for your business. Think about it, you can plan all day with people, and you can talk about what you are going to do, but there comes a point when you must do the job you discussed. The doing is the most time-consuming part and requires you to focus, which means that you might not have as much personal human interaction.

It can be especially lonely when you are first starting out and have no one except yourself to cheer you on and push your business forward. On top of that, you might have some critics who are doubting you and telling you that what you are trying to accomplish is impossible.

There is always going to be an element of loneliness as an entrepreneur because you have to think and work a lot, so you probably will not have much time for anything else at the beginning. That is okay though because you need your own space when you are trying to get established and figure out what decisions you need to make in order to work in a way that progresses your business. The high road is lonely, but it is worth it when you reach the other side.

Goal Setting

Part of being able to apply yourself and push your business every day is goal setting. The truth is that we do not always feel like working, but if you are able to set goals and do those small jobs that you do not necessarily enjoy, you will be able to keep your consistency in check. For instance, maybe you have a website and aim to get 400 visitors for a single month. If this is the case, you need to set a daily goal for the number of visitors you want to reach and see if it is feasible.

Goal setting keeps you motivated, and it holds you accountable because as you continue to set goals and reach them, you develop a mental habit that will discourage you from not attempting to meet your objectives. The push is all about getting to business and applying yourself to the various jobs that are necessary to complete if you want to get established as an entrepreneur. When you sit down and plan out your small goals in a manner that will allow you to use each one as a stepping stone to reach more prestigious goals, you will start to move forward with your business.

However, you must be careful that your goals are indeed moving you forward and not serving as mere busy work. This type of goal setting only serves the purpose of making you feel good about yourself for being "productive," but it really does not help you because instead of moving forward, you are wasting your energy by remaining stagnant. You would have been better off lying in bed and doing nothing because you would have had the same result.

As stated earlier, the entrepreneur game leaves no room for sympathy, and it does not care about your problems or circumstances. Either you show up to compete every single day, or you do not make it to the next level. To consciously set goals that do not help you move forward is just pure laziness, and instead of pushing the business, you are holding it back. There are so many great ideas that people have, but they fail because they do not set intelligent goals and end up burning out. However, if you are able to set quality objectives and develop the mentality that it is your obligation every single day to reach them, then even when you feel lazy, you will apply yourself because you will realize that the business will cease to move forward unless you push it in that direction.

Brain Power

Many people on social media will try to sell you a service and tell you that it is so simple to start making x amount of dollars with your store each month. However, some of these people do not want to emphasize the power you have within your mind. In fact, they want to make you feel as though you cannot accomplish your goals without them because at the end of the day, they are in business as well and looking for your dollar. You have the capacity to be able to turn your ideas into a business, but you need to always be thinking and using your mind to figure out what you can do behind the scenes in order to establish your following and grow your profits.

It is easy to get caught up in one strategy or one way of thinking, and if it works, keep doing it. However, the world changes quickly and often you have to change things about your business and brand development behind the scenes. As the entrepreneur, it is up to you to think about where you are now, where you are going, where you want to end up and how you will get there. However, thinking is not enough and your everyday decision to use your mind and intelligently execute on the behind the scenes functions of your business is what will bring you closer to your end goal each day.

Always remember that success is a scale, and there are many levels to it. If you sit for too long on past accomplishments, especially when you are not yet established in your industry, you will fall through and find yourself back at square one because the influence you built up is going to collapse. Do not be afraid to take a new approach to your business and change up your process.

Thinking is crucial when you are an entrepreneur, because if you are just going every single day and not thinking about the influence and impact of your business, you will end up falling behind to someone else that is using their mind. Look at the analytics and see what those numbers are telling you. The numbers do not lie, and you must use critical thinking skills in order to decide what direction you are going to move.

Are your analytics telling you to post more motivational videos instead of technical? It is all about realizing what is working, and if you find that something is bringing positive attention to your business, sit down and think of ways to continue exploring that concept.

To have a chance at becoming a successful entrepreneur, you need to use your mind and stop relying on the videos of people who are trying to take your money away. Videos are exceptional when you are using them for researching purposes and watching interviews to gain advice from successful minds, but when you are surfing the web and trying to look for someone to pay so that your business can get off the ground, you need to really think about what it is that you want. You will realize that you most likely will not have to pay a dime for expertise. Most of what you need to know in order to be successful is on the internet, or it is just a phone call or direct message away. Realize that success rests within your decision to think and execute on what you think about. Your business does not progress if your mind is not constantly thinking about how to improve and climb to the next level.

CHAPTER FIVE:

THE STAGES OF ENTREPRENEURSHIP

CHAPTER FIVE

Before deciding that you want to pursue entrepreneurship, you need to ask yourself if you are willing to dedicate to the rigorous process it demands of you. There is no security or guarantee that rests within this game, and all of the success depends on your actions and decisions. There are several stages to entrepreneurship, so it is no surprise that many fail when pursuing this path. There is an endless amount of reasons that people fail when trying to become an entrepreneur, but there is also a beautiful reward for those who last and make it through.

Idea

The first stage of entrepreneurship is the idea. The idea stage is one that we have all experienced a time or two before. As with any other thought that goes through your mind, it is easy to think of a theoretical situation that produces revenue and makes you rich overnight.

However, as you start to explore this idea more often and become interested, you start to realize that you do not know everything, and things are not as exact or easy as you had initially imagined. It is easy to get stuck in this stage and start to believe that you are further along than what you actually are. You have to be careful that you are not just merely discussing your ideas and remaining in denial about being more involved with them.

To succeed, you must experience this stage. Every reality was a thought before someone made it come to life, so dreaming about an idea is perfectly fine. Just make sure that once you decide you want to pursue this idea further, you do not get stuck with the mentality of thinking that "someday" it will happen. Someday never comes if you do not prepare yourself for the opportunity it has to offer. The idea stage is important because it gives you time to dream and develop drive.

Research

Once you have thought about the idea that you want to pursue, it is time to move on from that stage and begin your research to discover what you will need to know in order to get started. It is crucial to control your impulse, as some people would much rather jump in because they are too impatient to learn and educate themselves. That is what separates an entrepreneur who loves the industry from someone who just wants the shine, but you can save yourself a lot of time and mistakes if you do your homework beforehand.

There is so much depth to every lasting profitable idea. We can all set up fundraisers and have people donate to some cause, but to convert an idea from your mind into a tangible product is a whole different type of monster. Using your mind and researching the industry is critical to empowering your knowledge base. Skipping this stage without thinking can be very dangerous because it can result in you failing to actually know what your audience is looking for. Without proper research on your idea, it could take months or years to get yourself on the right track.

There are many ways you can go about researching your desired industry, but some of the best ways are simply watching videos of professionals and even setting up interviews with them. This can be intimidating at first, but what you have to realize is that your business and idea does not grow unless you grow. In order to develop your expertise and become a true entrepreneur, you must be willing to step out of your comfort zone for the sake of producing progress. Talking to professionals can be very beneficial because they can give you exceptional insight into what their processes consist of. This will motivate you to view your ideas from a realistic perspective. The more realistic and down to Earth your process and commitment becomes, the more likely you are to experience an eventual influx of massive success.

You must be patient during the research phase and hold yourself accountable so that you do not become lazy with your intake of information. It is impossible to know everything when you are first starting, but going in depth can only make you more knowledgeable. Knowledge is power, and the more you are willing to be quiet and listen, the more knowledge you will retain.

This stage of research should be looked at as an investment in your mind. If you were making an investment with your money, you would want to make sure that you were receiving the highest return possible. The same should apply when you invest your time and efforts into your research. You want to be able to acquire as much knowledge as possible, so you will be able to smoothly execute your ideas after your research. If you are going to rush anything when you are first getting started, it should be a rush to attain the most amount of knowledge possible. If you can do this, the rest will come. Master your art.

Establishment

Once you have taken the time to research your desired industry, you are ready to establish your business. Others might disagree with you and say you need x amount of dollars, or they might tell you that you need to have all of these other resources before you can start. Best advice? Do not listen. People will hold you back all day long with details and reasons as to why you cannot get started.

A real entrepreneur makes things happen for his/herself. Get started on developing the brand and functions of your business. Make social media accounts and lock them so that only you and those you trust have access to them. This will allow you to test ideas before unlocking the accounts and letting the world view them. You always want to be as polished as possible, and part of the establishment phase is setting yourself up for success before you decide to actually go live with the business and set its processes into motion.

During the establishment phase, you will want to be careful with who you allow to help you because some might not be rooting for you as much as they claim. You must be careful during this stage to not impatiently get your hopes up because you will be disappointed. There are plenty of people on the internet who will sell you excitement because they want you to pay them money in order to grow your sales by 10 times within 6 months or something along those lines. It is good to have people that will help you, but you have to be careful when taking advice like this because if you end up visiting this person's Instagram and notice that he/she has about two posts and 20k followers, then something is not right. More than likely, this individual paid for his/her followers in an effort to appear as credible and knowledgeable.

The reality is that entrepreneurship is an everyday hustle. You are full time if you are paying the bills, and people will tell you nowadays, "work smarter not harder." This is true to an extent, but these people that tell you this also understand the laziness and entitlement that has come with growing up in the internet age. With this understanding, they use it as a sell tactic and make you believe that you actually do not have to work that hard. It is not completely your fault if you do not have that same level of patience or natural work ability as the generations before you. However, you do need to be aware that hard work is definitely key to establishment, and if you think that you can lie to yourself about your work ethic or commitment and just jump right into business, you are in for a very rude awakening. The establishment stage comes with benefits because you are not actually in business yet, but instead you are able to appear as though you will be very successful.

As always though, time will tell you if you are truly an entrepreneur or if you were just a temporarily motivated individual. There is nothing wrong with seeking advice from professionals or experienced people who you trust, but when you are only seeking them for the quick buck and exciting ride, you will not be able to establish your foundation as a brand and business.

Survival

Once you have established your business and announced the grand opening, it is now time for reality to come and challenge you. This phase is where many people fail at entrepreneurship. You need grit to be a founder and owner of not just a business, but one that is growing, producing revenue and building relationships with customers. The survival stage can be difficult because you start to realize what is working and what is not working. The reality of the survival stage is that you will be grinding every single day in order to gain traction and grow your influence.

Grind

The realization of the grind that comes with the survival phase will come once the honeymoon feelings of opening your business and getting praise for the past few days has worn off. All successful businesses execute a process, and you will reach a point where your process starts to feel more like a job. This is not to say that you will become completely bored or tired of your job, but some days you might not have that same energy and excitement that you did when you first started. However, these processes that you follow everyday are what bring your business to the point of being able to satisfy your customers, so you must accept this as your job and something that you are obligated to complete. The ones who end up becoming successful entrepreneurs are the ones who first learn to survive.

Focus on Your Following

People fail during the survival phase because of the simple fact that they are not able to establish, maintain and grow a following. If you want to have a successful business, you need to focus on how your products/services can satisfy your customers. Why should they keep coming back to you? Some people fail to answer this question when starting their business, and because of that, they have a very great looking idea, but they have no revenue coming into their business.

During the survival phase, you will most likely not be able to have the privilege of being a full-time entrepreneur, so it is important that your actions are heavily emphasizing the growth of your influence and credibility. The way you do this is by communicating every single day with your following or with people you are trying to influence. Social media is a huge benefit in this instance, and you must use it if you want to empower your influence. When people view you as an influence, they will purchase your products/services.

Lack of Recognition

Another struggle during the survival phase is the lack of recognition you will receive. You have to think logically about this however, and realize that you are young with not many years of experience. You cannot blame people for not necessarily recognizing you right off the bat because there are many young individuals who pursue their ideas to a small extent but then end up losing their commitment. It is not normal to see a young person start his/her own business and actually have it become something successful. The way you can build this type of reputation for yourself is by understanding patience and consistency. You have to keep coming at them and showing the world what you are about.

Once they see that you are serious and pursuing this every single day, they will begin to respect you and hold you to a higher standard than they would the average young adult. There is a price that must be paid if you want to receive recognition for your work and dedication. That price is time and sacrifice. It can be easy to become discouraged during this time because you might feel afraid that you are starting to look foolish when your posts on social media are not getting hits, or maybe the people around you are just brushing your ideas off and not really paying you any mind. Nevertheless, this should serve as your motivation, and you need to believe in yourself during this time because that is the only way others will believe in you.

Front Lines

Moreover, while focusing on the behind the scenes processes and functions of your business is necessary to achieve entrepreneurial success, it is possible to focus too much on this aspect and neglect the front lines of your business; customers. If you are a passionate entrepreneur, you are probably very in love with your business and the functions that it entails. That is preferred, but you must remember that customers are the key to your entrepreneurial freedom, and if you neglect them, you will be shutting down.

You have to understand that your systems and processes are not going to be sad if you revert some of your attention from that aspect to your customers. However, your customers might feel discouraged or dissatisfied if you move your attention from them to your systems. There has to be a balance, and in the beginning, you will want to focus more on the customers because they are the ones who will be providing you the funds to keep your systems running. You can always be working on the behind the scenes aspect, but when it is time for customers, it is time for customers and nothing else.

Your focus does not necessarily need to be centered on the question of "How can I keep my customers happy?" Instead it needs to be "How can I solve my customer's problems?" An entrepreneur is a problem solver. This is not to say that you do not want the customer feeling happy about doing business with you, but if you are only focused on the aspect of happiness and not the actual job itself, then you will fall behind with your stream of revenue. Just because a customer visits your business and views your products/services does not mean that they will spend money. However, if you can show them how your product/service fixes their issue, you are more likely to have them purchase from your business.

This is why you must always be using your mind and thinking of how to serve as a benefit to the customer. You do not just want to be another addition to his/her happiness. Focus on targeting certain audiences and becoming a factor that progresses their lives in a better direction. You want to either become a necessity or get as close as you possibly can to seeming as one to your following.

Loneliness

Furthermore, another struggle that comes with the survival aspect is loneliness. You have to accept and adjust to being alone because as a young and ambitious entrepreneur, chances are that you will not find very many people who are willing to hang around all day and keep you company or help your business improve. This is why you must make sure that you are in a motivated and focused state of mind.

You have to remember why you started, or else you will end up falling off the edge and closing shop because you cannot handle the fact that you will have to be alone a lot of times during the beginning. However, as you continue to stick with your path and improve as an entrepreneur, you will produce profits and hopefully reach the point of being able to employ people or convince them to work closely with you. Either way, it can still be lonely because getting a business through the survival stage is very difficult work, and when you are being forced to invest the bulk of your focus into this aspect of life, it can cause you to become depressed and experience negative emotions.

The best thing you can do to help yourself cope with this reality is understand and accept that it is part of the game. You are definitely not alone because there are tons of successful entrepreneurs who have to endure this feeling. Your personal life is an important aspect and should not be ignored, so if that is healthy, you will be more likely to succeed in coping with the loneliness of entrepreneurship. Either way, you must accept this reality and understand that some people end up failing in the world of entrepreneurship because they cannot handle the aspect of loneliness. Being able to come to this realization should serve as motivation and give you purpose to not give up on your business or yourself.

Levels to Entrepreneurial Success

Moreover, the survival stage is difficult because there is still so much you have to learn about your industry, business and customers, but you must realize that there are levels to entrepreneurial success. If you are able to understand this and recognize what stage you are in, this knowledge will help you because it will serve as a sort of broad road map for gauging if you are truly heading in the right direction with your business.

Every single decision you make should serve the purpose of pushing your business from one level to the next. You cannot cheat the work ethic that genuine entrepreneurship requires if you want to actually develop a business that produces profit and solves problems for customers on a regular basis. Your brand and business will not be recognized if you do not execute and make the proper decisions to put your business in a position to be recognized.

However, you must be patiently impatient when moving your business from one level to the next. What this means is that you have to be impatient in the sense that you need to be working every single day on your process in order to push the business forward. However, you also need to be patient in the sense that you realize it is going to take you time to fully develop and grow your business to the extent that you desire. This extent never comes to fruition if you are not executing every day and moving up levels.

Managing Your Schedule

In addition to understanding the significance of levels in entrepreneurship, another key aspect of in this game is knowing how to properly manage your schedule so that you are completing the necessary amount of each day. You might be a college student or in the workforce, and if this is the case, you must be careful with how you manage your time because it can prove a difficult task to stay on top of your business. It is very easy to get home from school or work, or even both, and say to yourself that you are going to head straight to bed. However, while that is the healthier take on life, if you are up for the challenge to add entrepreneurship to your workload, you must create time for that every single day. Think wisely. Maybe your strongest time of the day is the morning, so that could be an indication for you to wake up earlier than usual in order to get some business done and decrease your end of day workload.

It might even be best to type or write out your daily schedule on a spreadsheet because this will help ensure that your work will be completed each day and erase the anxiety of having too much responsibility. It is easy to feel overwhelmed about your workload, but when you take the time to enter it into a spreadsheet, you realize that as long as you can focus during the allotted time slots, you will finish tasks much more efficiently and feel better upon completion of each one.

Knowing how to manage your schedule properly will allow you to have a healthier and stronger approach towards taking on your business during the survival stage. One cannot consistently go without an adequate amount of sleep for a long duration of time and still perform at exceptional standards. As ambitious and driven as you may feel at the time you are planning your schedule, be realistic when you integrate tasks and breaks.

No one can work straight through a whole day with absolutely no breaks of some type. If you do this, you will end up falling off track of the schedule, and it will not be long before you completely abandon it and become an ineffective time manager. Breaks are essential because they give you time to rest and allow you to become motivated. You need motivation in order to execute your tasks to the most intelligent and quality extent possible. The healthier you are, the better you will perform as an entrepreneur.

What Does/Does Not Work?

During the survival stage, even though you might have educated yourself about the industry you are in, you still have so much to learn, but only experience is going to teach you these lessons. As an entrepreneur, you will want to try new things and get creative to see just how far you can go to make something as exceptional as possible. This can be a process, system, customer telephone script, etc.

You must use trial/error as an entrepreneur, and you cannot fear failure. In fact, you need to expect failure throughout your entire life because it will continue to happen over and over again, but if you are able to learn why you failed and what you can do to improve, you will see that aspect of your business flourish each time.

It is especially important to continually try new things as an entrepreneur because what is in style today could very well be outdated tomorrow. We have social media and smartphones, so a new trend could hit the globe immediately and impact the performance and perception of your business. However, for the most part, while you should expect change and not feel too surprised by any urgent trends, the survival stage will allow you to find out what works for you in terms of processes, systems and procedures. Once you find what works for you, it is all about consistency and quality. You will continue to struggle and deal with change, but for every target audience there is a sweet spot that triggers them to buy your products/services.

Maintaining Motivation and Creativity

Boredom comes with any business regardless if you are the most passionate about it or completely despise it. It is just part of being human, but you have to find it within yourself every single day to remember that same motivation you had before you started. It is not always easy to go about feeling motivated when you are young and realize that you are missing out on a lot, but that is part of maturing and understanding that you are competing with giant corporations ran by prestigious professionals.

You have to acknowledge your boredom and lack of motivation when it hits you, but when you are serious and treating your idea as an actual place of business, you begin to develop habits and feelings of accountability to not only complete tasks but also innovate.

Creativity is huge as an entrepreneur, and you cannot be afraid to express yours. Every successful entrepreneur is creative in his/her own manner because this person was able to see a need for his/her idea and implement it in a way that was profitable. Taking time to observe your business and think about what else it could use in order to not only increase profits, but first and most importantly, your customer base, is essential to your survival as a business.

Understand that you are the entrepreneur and mind behind this business that your audience craves. Knowing this will give you more confidence to be creative and implement new ideas. Also, with creativity comes happiness and fulfillment. If you are able to think of a unique procedure or product that can solve customer problems more efficiently, you will gain confidence in your ways of thinking. However, you must not become conceited and think that everything you touch will turn into gold. That type of thinking is a fast track to entitlement and will eventually lead you to failure.

It can be so difficult to get through the survival stage and prosper, but it can also be all too easy to lose your business in a matter of seconds because of a foolishly prideful and impulsive decision. If you use a creative idea and have success, you can appreciate and celebrate it, but never sit on any accomplishment. The clock is moving and so is the relevance of your prior accomplishments and current thoughts. If you are able to maintain motivation and creativity during the survival phase, you will find it easier to endure because you will feel happier.

Originality

Being yourself is a very critical aspect of successful entrepreneurship because while you can paint an image for the public to fall in love with, you will be much happier overall if you are able to use your self-awareness as a guide to find your target audience. If your following is satisfied and influenced by who you are as a person, there is a big weight that is taken off your shoulders. It will be easier to feel confident in your decisions, and you will be more respected. Entrepreneurship that is built to last and remain relevant throughout time is built off of authenticity. If you are one to follow the trends and be a slave to every single change, your values and principles could potentially get messed up, and you might fail to maintain a loyal following. People want to follow the original. No one wants to follow someone's clone or a wannabe because there is no genuine influence within that.

The survival stage can be difficult for any entrepreneur who is trying to express his/her originality because this person has not yet seen this aspect turn into recurring profits or a large sphere of inspirational influence. However, the key to creating a large sphere of influence is being able to remain original on a consistent basis. In a way, you have to force society to accept your uniqueness on a gradually increasing scale. What this means is that you have to keep coming at the world with products, services and content. If you are able to do this, you will eventually break the mold and find the system becoming more accepting of your business.

When you are young, it will be more difficult for you to have credibility and respect professionally, but if you continue at this age to pursue your ideas from a mature and original point of view, it will only be a matter of time until the rest of the world catches on. That is not to say that you must not take the necessary actions to gain recognition, but the larger your catalog of work, the more credible you will become. You must remain original during the tough stage of survival because this will result in a better set up for long-term success and happiness.

Furthermore, the survival stage comes with a great amount of struggle and realization. It is the stage where you truly discover who you are as a person, brand, business and influencer. Do not become discouraged when embracing your uniqueness and remember to stay consistent with your values, principles and work ethic. Always solve the customer's problems with integrity and respect.

Hypergrowth

The stage of hypergrowth is achieved once your idea has proven to produce profits to the extent of conquering the challenges of surviving. During this stage, your business starts to grow at an exponential rate, and although money is coming in, it is important that you do not get too comfortable or satisfied with your success. You are not at your peak yet, and you still cannot compete with the big players in your industry. Nevertheless, you have made a name for yourself at this point, and you are on a potential path to the top of the ladder. It is all about levels, and your focus still needs to be aligning your variables in a manner that progress your business.

Rapid Pace

During hypergrowth, your business begins to grow at a rapid pace because you have established a strong and loyal following through unique and personalized strategies that have produced sustainable and recurring profits. Difficulties can arise during this stage because if you are growing at a fast pace, you might need to allocate the workload to a larger number of individuals, which would indicate that you will have to put the time and effort into searching for more employees. Nevertheless, if your business makes it to the hypergrowth phase, you are in for an exciting ride, but this excitement must be maintained as you have still not peaked.

Throughout this time, you will gain a new and more rapid following, but you will also gain more critics, so it is important that you stay consistent with the fundamentals of your business. Doing so will allow you to maintain a consistent and original identity while also growing at an exponential pace.

According to a study done by World Economic Forum, the top three focuses of hypergrowth companies were scalability, talent and technology. As stated earlier, there are levels to entrepreneurial success, and those who view their decisions as a means to get from one level to the next end up experiencing the largest amount because they are focused on constant upward progression. Entrepreneurs who become comfortable with a certain level of achievement end up stagnating and eventually declining because not only are they not trying to stay ahead of the game, but they are leaving themselves open to various vulnerabilities by not adapting to the constant changes in today's fast-moving society.

Now, while the concentration of scaling up to different levels of success should be the central focus, this is extremely difficult to accomplish if the level of talent is not in sync with the required amount for the ultimate vision. One might ask the question of, "How can you gauge if the level of talent is adequate?" The answer to this is growth. Is the employee able to grow with the company and also contribute to its growth? The answer to these questions will tell you if the level of talent is in sync with the mission of maintaining hypergrowth.

Different positions require different levels and types of talent, but if you are filling executive positions, you will want to make sure that you are recruiting the most intelligent and driven talent possible. These are the people who will be making decisions that determine the direction of the business. However, you will also want to set standards and requirements in order to uphold a high employee talent level, but you must be careful because you want your workers to feel happy and intrinsically motivated when working in their assigned positions.

Talent is one standard, but as an employer you must make sure that you are putting forth the most necessary amount of effort to ensure that your employees remain happy while working. As long as work results are improving, you should not stop trying to provide incentives and rewards for employees in order to make their jobs more pleasurable. This will benefit you and your employees by bringing out their best performance and strengthening your rapport with them.

Moreover, while scaling and talent were top priorities of hypergrowth companies, technology was another key focus.

With modern day technology, companies are able to expand into a variety of different markets at the same time. Being able to execute the functions of technology in a manner that is parallel to this reasoning is crucial to succeeding during the hypergrowth phase because without it, you might find yourself at a huge disadvantage in comparison to your competitors. It is because of technology that some of the news being released at this moment is already irrelevant.

Before anyone ever reads or writes the news, someone else already knows about it. To properly execute technology, you need a team who specializes in it because you cannot manage such a time consuming and crucial responsibility on your own. During hypergrowth, business is too fast, and you alone are not enough to manage that caliber of labor. Properly executing technology in order to stay ahead and understand trends is critical to maintaining your business during hypergrowth.

Stability

During the hypergrowth phase, one of your key goals is stability. This is maintained by understanding the extent of application that must be invested into the business from employees to technology. Stability is achieved by educating yourself about how large of a scope your business is currently covering and where it is heading based off of the analytics provided to you via social media platforms or other statistical records. Once you have a research team that is willing to dig deep into your business and industry to identify trends, this will allow you to focus on your role as the entrepreneur and promote stability for your business. Stability must be achieved before you can reach your prime stage of entrepreneurship. It is still very possible that your business can fall through and fail, so you must not only focus on moving forward but also building the stable foundation of support for your business to continue developing from.

To be more specific, you need to know that the people working around you are dependable. The more people you lose during hypergrowth, the more difficult it will become to maintain the quality of your business. For instance, if you end up losing a director for your social media content, you will need to know who is going to replace that person. You cannot get comfortable with the new and more successful circumstances because as the Notorious B.I.G. stated, “mo money mo problems.” That is a very real statement because as your business grows, your involvement becomes more serious, and people start to depend on you for necessities.

Your employees depend on you to pay them in order to support their families, and your customers depend on you to continue delivering quality products/services as an answer to their wants and needs. Being able to depend on your team is very important because this is what provides you the stability to continue taking care of all stakeholders of your business.

Manage Your Ego

At heart, many entrepreneurs are very competitive, but managing your ego is a must if you want to maximize your business’ productivity and growth. This is where maturity of your entrepreneurial mind must come around and realize that your success is not about you, but it is instead about the people purchasing from you. We get trapped inside of our ego at times when we experience a great amount of success. To appreciate the hypergrowth of your business is necessary, but to become arrogant and overconfident is all too familiar with the story of pride coming before the fall. Learn from others who have failed because of their ego, and use their stories as a lesson to not let yours get too large. If you have time to think about how amazing you are, you are not investing enough time into your business. An ego can become damaging as an entrepreneur because while you might feel as though you are something special, failure is inevitable, and you will find yourself just as damaged as you were excited.

Prime

Once your business has conquered the stages of survival and hypergrowth, it will then be in its most powerful and respected form; its prime. As an entrepreneur, you will want to keep your business in its prime for as long as possible. It is this stage that many work to reach but a lot less actually achieve.

During the prime stage, a business is fully and properly functional in all of its departments. There is no longer a massive struggle of any sort to find a dedicated group of employees. All members of every department are being paid at a proper and consistent rate, and your business is able to take care of those who are running it.

Moreover, because your business has developed a loyal following, steady paychecks and a dependable team, you now have more room for innovation. This will allow your business to venture into other industries in order to continue its growth and creation of jobs for a broader demographic. You could also inspire younger entrepreneurs and businesses to take on a new approach towards your industry. A good example of venturing into other industries would be Amazon's decision to purchase Whole Foods. As a business that is publicly traded in the Internet and Direct Marketing Retail industry, it was an unusual decision by Amazon to purchase a company in the groceries industry.Innovation is key to growth and relevance in the world of business, and when you are in the prime stage, you have the capabilities to develop new perspectives for your company.

Another benefit that comes with the influence and respect of the prime stage is the ability to establish partnerships and new businesses. As a powerful corporate entity, in order to keep the fear of takeover or loss of market share at bay, some businesses will partner with others that are relative to its industry. An entrepreneur can also use his/her business to acquire or start a new business. Again, using Amazon as an example, its founder, Jeff Bezos, has a startup space business known as Blue Origin. It is because of Amazon's financial success that Bezos has not only become the world's richest human being, but he is also able to join the space race in an attempt to reach Mars. The ability of a business to create partnerships and start new, respectable companies will allow it to maintain its prime stage relevance and performance.

Decline

The decline stage can be defined as one where your business starts to become less relevant in its industry. During this period, you might lose partnerships, market share and credibility. The reason partnerships could be lost is because these businesses could either be going bankrupt, closing shop or making a move to partner with a younger and more promising company. On top of this, if you are a publicly traded business, you will see the stock price for your business decrease as investor sentiment becomes more and more pessimistic about the ability of your business to thrive in the coming years.

The world is always evolving, and as an entrepreneur, if you cannot adapt and accept that there is a new age who is innovating and coming up with a more clever and convenient way to compete with your business, you will experience a decrease in market share. A decreasing market share means that you are losing influence.

As an entrepreneur, you need influence because this is what urges your audience to purchase your products and services. With a loss of influence comes a loss of credibility. Yes, you might have been the best at one point and known a lot about the industry and its concepts. However, the game is always changing in terms of systems and communication. Part of the decline stage is the fact that your business loses credibility and begins to become irrelevant to the newer generations. If you cannot accept the fact that old ways do not last, you will lose as an entrepreneur. Do not stay attached to a certain way of doing things.

CHAPTER SIX:

THE TIME FACTOR

CHAPTER SIX

When you are young, it is more difficult to realize the value and importance of time. 20 years old might seem so young, but if you are really trying to become a force on a large scale, you cannot take your time for granted. So many people waste their most healthy and able years contemplating on success instead of actually waking up, stepping out of their comfort zone and making those day to day actions that would help them grow as a person and entrepreneur. These individuals tell themselves, “I am going to make it,” or “I am going to get to business and start grinding.” This might last for a night or two, but it goes away very quickly, and it is because of this that they will watch their dreams slip away from them.

Time passes you by, and you do not even realize it until you are almost 30 years old and working a job you did not dream about. Depending on your audience and the industry you wish to pursue, you might even find that your relevance window is closing dramatically because you have grown too out of touch with the functioning of your audience to connect with them. However, when you were 20 you were enjoying your life while sitting on your ego and entitlement that you received from the teachers during grade school and college, but that destroyed your dreams, and you became a mere constituent of the world. You have to know how to produce income on a regular basis as an entrepreneur in order to be able to pay the bills. 20 years old is an extremely important time in your life, and if you cannot be responsible and disciplined enough to realize this, your business will not witness growth.

Nothing moves if you are not moving, so that is why every single day must be valued as an addition to your larger vision. It takes years to scale up and gain credibility in the game because there are so many people like you who are temporarily taking up the space and fading away, which proves that they did not have what it took to be able to make a name and compete with the corporate executives who have access to all the money one could imagine. Understanding the value of right now is key to truly progressing your business.

Living in Your Mind

Something we learn to do growing up is dream about how great we can make our lives if we truly work hard and apply ourselves. It is very easy to create your own sense of entitlement and truly start to believe that you are meant for greater circumstances than those in front of you. However, your thoughts do not determine this, but instead it is your actions. We spend so much time thinking about the future when we are growing up that we learn to only think and not actually apply. This becomes a problem when you get out on your own as a young person with entrepreneurial aspirations because you have no sense of reality when it comes to turning your business ideas into a source of revenue.

In order to become that singer, author or business owner that you wanted to become when you were younger, you need to stop living in your mind and start making physical moves that actually sets tangible objects into motion. This is what will integrate correct energy into the world that will lead to your business ideas becoming more and more real with every decision you make.

There are way more “wantrepreneurs” than entrepreneurs on this planet, and this happens for various reasons such as insecurity, laziness, negative responses to circumstances, etc. Some people who make fun of you and insult your vision or do not take you seriously actually have their own aspirations, but they are so insecure with themselves that they do not even think about actually making a real decision to set their goals into motion. These people are so worried about what their peers and elders will think of them that they are completely paralyzed when it comes to pursuing their ideas. This leads to them settling for a secure job that they really did not want, but that is the position that insecurity led them to. A secure job is good to have, and maybe you do enjoy it, but if you are a young soul and aspiring entrepreneur reading this, then you have to do this for you. You cannot live your life tied down by preferences of what you should or should not do. You get one life in human history, and if you are living as a crippled soul that cannot discuss his/her dreams, your very short window of life is going to close, and you will be buried never knowing what could have been.

Your approach to how you handle your insecurities of discussing your ideas means a great deal, especially when you are young and do not have hardly anything except an idea and ambition. If you are going to be an entrepreneur, you have to accept criticism because it will always exist and attempt to make you feel discouraged. There will always be someone calling you a fool or saying you should not do this or that. However, they are not you, and that is why you naturally and rightfully should do things your way and not theirs. You are the entrepreneur of your business, and you are the one with the most in-depth vision, so it almost makes no sense to listen to degrading criticism.

It is one thing to be insecure, but to be lazy is another absolute killer of dreams, and the truth is that entrepreneurship is very difficult when you are starting out. You may think you are working enough, but results are going to tell you the real answer to that question.

Growing up without a sense of reality can be damaging as an aspiring entrepreneur because there are a lot of us who do not have to worry about paying bills or buying groceries when we are young. Adolescence is different because you are eligible to get a job and pay for certain things in order to help yourself and the people taking care of you. However, you will find that the habits you develop as a young person only grow stronger as you get older, and this can either be detrimental or beneficial to your progression as an entrepreneur. It is amazing how some individuals can dream so largely and believe for a second that they will have such a rewarding career, but yet this person is only working when they feel like it.

People on the internet encourage you to work smarter instead of harder, but the truth is that if you do not have hustle, you will not last. Hustle is the key to success. It beats intelligence and knowledge because while you can know a lot and be a smart person, if you are not applying that, it is all going to waste. However, the person who hustles is going to learn by experience if not anything else, and it is for this reason that he/she is going to experience a successful breakthrough. If you develop lazy habits, no one who is of value in business is going to want anything to do with you or your idea. Show that you value today by the way you go about hustling.

Lastly, there are people who have dreams and really want to be entrepreneurs, but what they do is immediately destroy their potential by using their unpleasant circumstances as an excuse. If you are a true entrepreneur, you will run through a brick wall to make sure that your ideas are manifested into this world. There is not a single thing that you will let get in your way. Now, there are challenges that are extremely difficult to deal with and it could lead to you needing a time of rest and self-reflection. However, it is that entrepreneurial fire in your soul that is going to force your place in this world to make sure you get paid to live out your dreams. We have seen people come from the worst of situations and still be able to experience the American Dream because of their decision to respond like a champion to seemingly defeating circumstances. As an entrepreneur, you have to have the mentality that says, "I have no idea how to go about doing this, but I am just going to do it." That right there is what makes an entrepreneur successful. You must be a creator of your circumstances and not a victim of them.

Entrepreneurship is all about freedom, and you cannot be free if you are always acting as a slave to your circumstances. Every single person has the potential to become something greater than what is in front of him/her, but it is up to each person to respond in a manner that screams champion.

Content

Another very important aspect of understanding the value of right now is realizing the importance of creating and distributing content. This is what shows people that you are an initiator of your word who means business. Do you think that these artists you listen to would be anywhere if they released little to no content at all? The answer is no because if this were the case, no one would have heard them. Also, if someone heard that a certain entrepreneur released one piece of content and looked this up to find that nothing else ever followed, that "entrepreneur" would immediately lose the little credibility that he/she had.

In order to keep your influence progressing, you must create content. When you are starting out, you are trying to get noticed by the correct people. If you are holding content back as if you were a huge star, this will only slow you down because not very many people know you, so there is nothing that too many people are getting excited about.

When it comes to content, you have to take the patiently impatient approach. This means that you must try to distribute as much content as possible every single day, but have the patience to know that even when you feel that you have created and distributed so much content, you might have not even broken the surface yet. It is all about understanding and respecting the current state of your business. If you want to be that big-time entrepreneur, you have to work like he/she would. However, while your work ethic needs to represent that of a successful entrepreneur, your entitlement needs to be turned to zero because the reality is that your content is not yet respected or seen as being on the same level as massively successful entrepreneurs.

Creating and distributing quality content will bring respect and credibility to your brand and business because you will not only start to develop a loyal following, but you will also start to become noticed by people in your industry. Your following needs something to hold onto and take in. If all you give them is one piece and get lazy, they are going to grow tired of you, especially when you are just starting out.

Business Plan

If you do not have one already, you will need to create a business plan because without a guide to go by, you will not know what functions to initiate every day, or you will get comfortable with your current process and limit yourself from exploring new and beneficial opportunities. A business plan allows you to structure your business in a variety of ways from job positions and roles to setting standards of growth to reach. As a business, you want to see your influence grow because this will result in revenue growth. However, if you do not have a plan, you can only continue for so long until you reach a level of success that forces you to realize you are lost because you do not have a goal to work towards. You never want your business to become stagnant because that means some people are catching up and/or passing you.

The first step to creating a business plan is understanding the current stage you are in. If you are reading this, you are most likely in the idea, establishment or survival stage. You will be able to decide which phase you are in based off of the characteristics of your circumstances as a business. You must know your current state in order to have growth. To put things into perspective, think about your life. Right now, you might be in high school or college, and you are looking at where you are in order to determine what you need to do to get to where you want to end up. Likewise, when you are a business, you need to look at your current circumstances in order to determine the stage you are associated with.

CHAPTER SEVEN:

INVENTING YOUR ENTREPRENEURIAL IDENTITY

CHAPTER SEVEN

The ability to create influence and exposure as an entrepreneur are key skills because without these defining characteristics, you will not be able to produce sales or grow your following. In doing this, you are inventing your entrepreneurial identity because you want to be able to sell your audience on your image. Social media is the main stage for creating your identity, and you must use it in a way that exposes the aspects of yourself that would be desirable to your target audience. In order to develop an image and maintain its status, you must stay dedicated and open minded to what is relevant.

Developing Your Image

Your image is crucial to your influence and flow of revenue because when you are targeting a certain demographic of people, the image has to satisfy this group. It is too easy to overlook this aspect when you are first beginning because you will be inevitably naïve. However, if you have not developed an image for your audience to become attached to, you will eventually notice because your business and hustle will be stellar, but there will be no unique theme that relates to your followers.

In order to create your image, you need to first focus on the home page of all of your social media accounts. In this day and age, you have to have two businesses if you want to be an entrepreneur; your product/service and your social media marketing hustle. Every aspect, such as your homepage, header, profile picture, bio, etc. needs to serve the purpose of attracting your target audience. If newcomers are able to view your profile and become hooked on the content, they will follow you because they will want to see more. You must be careful when constructing your homepage because you want to make sure that it relates to your target audience as much possible. Spotting potential issues can be difficult as the entrepreneur because you have so much going through your mind, so it would help to discuss the demographics with your peers and get their honest opinions on how well you are representing the correlation between your homepage and target audience.

Another important aspect of developing your image as an entrepreneur is the way you go about setting up your website. You need to make sure that the theme of the website and social media homepages are in unison and support the same values. If your target audience is hooked on your social media pages, they will most likely visit your website (if you choose to create one), and if the content is not similar, they will notice and become dissatisfied and/or confused. This is the last thing you want, so again, ask your peers and other credible individuals to view your website for assurance.

Moreover, your website needs to clearly indicate what it is that your business does. Be cautious to not get so caught up in the creative side that you accidentally make your products/services difficult to find. Not only does this irritate site visitors, but it also makes you look unprofessional. For instance, if you have a lawn mowing service, there needs to be pictures clearly depicting this and easily identifiable tabs offering services. The organizational aspect of your website is extremely important to the way your business is perceived, and you cannot create a positive perception with a poorly organized site.

Likewise, not only is the type of content you post on social media important, but the intent behind why you post the content is key to getting proper results. For instance, just creating a beautifully designed picture with a quote is not going to cut it. Yes, it is content, and you will see results, but before you post it, you need to know why you are posting the picture. Do you want followers? Do you want website hits? Are you wanting likes and shares? Deciding what you want out of each post will develop you into a master of your social media craft because you will know exactly what, when, why and for whom it works. Always be willing to experiment and look foolish in the name of progress. Decide why you are posting something and try to predict the results you will receive before making the post. The more you do this, the better you will be able to understand your audience.

Maintaining Your Image

Once you have developed your image, you will need to learn how to stay consistent, but also make sure your audience does not become bored with you. There have been countless entrepreneurs in various industries that have blown up one year and blown out the next. This happened because their foundation was not strong enough. It is one thing to develop a foundation for your image, but it is another to keep your influence relevant for the long-run. We see artists such as Jay-Z and Kanye West who have been around for more than two decades and are able to stay not only relevant but important to upcoming generations. This is because they have mastered the art of maintaining their entrepreneurial identities.

As time progresses, changes will occur, but it is up to you to adapt in a way that is influential and relevant. The way you do this is by studying the current leaders of your industry. You might become upset because you notice that up and coming entrepreneurs in your spectrum do not have much depth but are receiving all of the attention. That is okay because what you can do with this is take the swag of the brand or business that is currently hot and ingrain it within certain products of your company. For instance, maybe you have a clothing brand that sells urban wear. You might notice that someone else in your industry is profiting heavily from creating shirts that are similar to yours, but the material being used is different and cheaper. If this is the case, keep the style, but change the material of your shirt and see what happens.

However, you must be careful during this time because you want to maintain your loyal following. Instead of changing a shirt completely, you could perhaps create a completely new shirt that has the same style but new material. If successful, not only could you retain your initial following, but you could also benefit them if they enjoy the new material. In order to maintain your image, you must be able to adapt in a relevant and influential manner.

CHAPTER EIGHT:

PATIENTLY IMPATIENT

CHAPTER EIGHT

One of the difficulties of being a young entrepreneur is the fact that you have to learn patience. Being patient is more difficult today than it ever was before thanks to technological innovation and the internet's speedy means of almost instantly connecting us to the rest of the world. The waiting game is not one that is necessarily enjoyable, and when you add some long nights and a lack of social life to the mix, it can become even more difficult. However, the reality is that the success of your business might require this behavior. In order to generate enough income that will consistently pay you and others, you will need to invest the proper amount of time and energy into your process.

Moreover, since you cannot yet pay yourself and your bills, you will probably have to work a job either full-time or part-time, and on top of that, you might even be a high school or college student. If this is the case, it might be very difficult to maintain a complete social life if you want to take your business seriously and commit to your due diligence. In order to have success and see growth as a young entrepreneur, you must become patiently impatient with your work.

Indeed, as stated earlier, patience can be difficult in this day and age because we have the privilege of using advanced technological innovations, but as an entrepreneur, you must have a long-term outlook for growth and build your foundation in a very caring manner. Understand that you will not become rich maybe even ten years from when you started. It all depends on your business and the way you go about executing your process. If you are going into business with the mentality that things are going to speedily pick up and you will gain all of this credibility and money, you might be in for a rude awakening. Having huge expectations is a very easy thing to do, but it will not be too long before reality sets in and you realize that you missed out on a lot of important details.

This is an obvious concept when thinking about it, but when you are in the moment, the excitement is inevitable, and no matter how down to Earth you want your mind to stay, there will be an added kick of excitement at the beginning. The key is to control it so that it serves as a benefit and tool for growth rather than a detriment. You want this excitement to always last in the back of your mind because that is what will fuel your passion every single day. However, you need to think of your everyday actions as an investment into the future direction of your business. To not value today is to not value the days ahead of you. If you think success is ahead in the future, but you are disappointed because you did not meet the sky-high expectations for yourself within a few months, you will not know how to value your days and truly invest in yourself.

If your dream is to build a large and lasting business or career like Nike or rap artist, Jay-Z, you need to go into your business with not only a long-term state of mind, but one that is attentive to detail. The goal when you are beginning is to build a strong, loyal and stable following that will support you and get excited about the future of your business. The establishment of something like this starts with the little details that add to your credibility. For instance, if you are creating social media posts (unless it is part of your brand to misspell words), make sure that every single word is properly spelled. Pay attention to the quality of the pictures you are posting on your profiles. If you reply to a post comment, do not merely say "thank you" and go along with your day. It is called social media for a reason, so visit that person's page in order to be able to make a genuine reply that is specific to his/her business.

So many people get lazy and start sending generic mass messages that are no different than the other countless ones before them. This might be a red flag to not do business with this person because he/she is not really showing true interest in you or your business. He/she might just want your money, and because you do not know this person, he/she could be a scammer as well. Be cautious of how you choose to associate with people when conducting your business. You cannot cheat the hustle of entrepreneurship. In order to have longevity you must be patient and focus on the small details.

However, while you do want to focus on small details, this is not to say that you should let them dominate your vision to the point of crippling the progression of your business. Putting too much thought into the small details will waste your energy and motivation, which will lead to your business underperforming. Having a team would help in this sense because the attention to detail can be allocated among certain members. You want to make sure that you have a deep understanding of your business and its products, but as the entrepreneur you are also the ambassador for your business. This means that you need to spend time communicating with people that can collaborate with you or help you develop value in different aspects.

When you are always focusing on the small details of your products/services to the point of exhaustion, you start to become dull. This can serve as a detriment to you as the ambassador because it prevents you from working on your communication skills. Details are very important and necessary when developing a lasting business, but do not let them drain you of motivation and energy because you need that in order to expand.

Nevertheless, understanding the concept of what it means to become patiently impatient will serve as a huge benefit to your entrepreneurial journey. Once you realize how much time you have and also the value within the time, you will be able to focus on your business everyday while having feasible expectations for yourself. Entrepreneurship is not a guaranteed success, but if you can take the time to master your craft day in and day out, it might only be a matter of time until you reap the success that you have been craving.

CHAPTER NINE:

REJECTION

CHAPTER NINE

Get used to it. In the world of entrepreneurship, especially when you are young and just beginning, you are going to get rejected time and time again. Part of being an entrepreneur is being able to consistently but properly deal with rejection and criticism. The reality is that people will pat you on the back and stand behind you, but eventually you might find that this comfort becomes pretty useless, and until you are able to really establish something that is disruptive in your industry, you will not get many serious looks. Learning how to deal with rejection is crucial to the life of your business because depending on your response, your business either will or will not survive.

Straight Rejection

The feeling of total rejection is one that needs to be dealt with carefully because you do not want to hurt your self-esteem, reputation or burn bridges. Indeed, if you are young and have a business, the chances are that when you tell an adult about it, you more than likely will not get the credit you feel you deserve. In fact, depending on who you speak with, you might get completely rejected and told that your idea is going to fail. However, this is a mere opinion, and whether you have a professional talking with you or not, the approach this person takes towards expressing his/her opinion will tell you if it is foolish bias or if the criticism is constructive and backed by necessary reasoning.

What you must realize is that this is the age of social media. Who knows social media better than this generation? That is correct. No other does, and because of this, you are placed on the exact same playing field as those who appear to be "above" you. We no longer need large amounts of capital to become successful entrepreneurs. That is not to say that having large capital is not a huge advantage, but what we do have is the ability to hustle and use our minds. When backed with a determined state of mind, our energy can handle any type of rejection or criticism.

A problem that some of us have is that when we face rejection, we completely shut down or lose confidence in ourselves and our ideas. Shutting down when you are just starting should be nowhere on your list. All opportunity and feedback should be heard, but if it serves the purpose of telling you to shut down or making you feel as if the odds are so against you that your goal is impossible, all you need to do is look at the aspects that need the most amount of improvement and execute accordingly.

Never let any person who is experienced or wealthy allow you to feel disempowered. You are a boss when you wake up and determine it in your mind. This is not to say that you should not show class and have respect for people with more experience, but it is saying that you have just as much of a right to becoming a successful entrepreneur as your peers and elders if you are willing to learn and stay relentless regardless of failure or rejection.

"Great Job" Kid

This may not seem as rejection to some, but when you think about it, one who is merely telling you "great job" and immediately losing interest is really not impressed and is only categorizing you as something that has already been seen before. As human beings, it is very easy to reply in a way that only serves the purpose of keeping the messenger happy, and this is why people will reject you with a hot air compliment. When you experience this, it can be irritating because a genuine entrepreneur, old or young is a very dedicated and hardworking individual. However, while this is true, you have to realize that most people are not going to be anywhere near as enthusiastic about your idea as you, especially if the person you are discussing your idea with does not benefit in any way. Because of this, you should not feel discouraged when someone is passively complimenting you.

On top of that, you should not even be seeking out compliments but rather honest reviews. We love to be praised and recognized for our work, but we grow when we are given realistic and constructive feedback. It can be irritating to have to hear what you did wrong, but when you know that the person giving you constructive criticism is doing it for your benefit, you need to take a step back and really consider the suggestions being presented to you.

Take it as a grain of salt when someone seems to push you to the side because that is a major aspect of being a young or new entrepreneur. If you let this destroy your confidence, you will not be able to efficiently execute your business idea.

"You Have a Long Way to Go"

This is the indirect way of telling you that you should basically just forget about your dreams and submit to the ways of society. Now, be careful because sometimes you actually do have a long way to go. However, you can tell if the person telling you this is truly trying to help you or just getting you out of his/her presence. Tone, the types of comments used and body language will communicate much of this.

Also, if the person you are seeking feedback from is really not providing you with much logical reasoning, you should take the initiative to end the conversation immediately because it is a waste of your time. There can be a certain level of entitlement that exists within someone's mind when you ask him/her to help you, and this is what causes that person to talk down on you rather than help. Do not be afraid to respectfully end a conversation that is only serving the purpose of suppressing your potential.

Indirect rejection should serve as not only motivation, but a development of accountability to ensure that your business processes are being executed efficiently in every aspect. One reason that people will not take you serious as a young entrepreneur is because they might have experience in an industry related to your business and are able to see all of the moving parts within that company.

It is uncommon that someone who is young takes the initiative to truly commit to his/her idea as an employee would his/her job. However, this is what you must do as an entrepreneur, and you need to be constantly looking for ways to grow and expand your influence. Once you start to wrap your mind around this point, you become more mature, and the more mature your business becomes, the more respected and relevant you become to other businesses and consumers.

CHAPTER TEN:

TEAM BUILDING

CHAPTER TEN

Strong team building is at the core of every business that eventually becomes a successful corporation. If you think about large businesses such as Nike, Facebook, Apple, etc. you will notice that these are now large corporations that started with one or very few more entrepreneurs who took the initiative to build a team. If your plan is to eventually take your ideas to the highest level, you will need to have the assistance from others in order to get there. While building a team can seem like a daunting challenge, you will find that at some point, it is inevitable that you will have to build one if you plan on having major long-term success as a large corporation.

Naturally, when some of us think of entrepreneurship, we think of all the tasks that we as individuals must complete in order to progress our business. This can lead to various problems such as anxiety, a lack of productivity and a lack of proper input. It is for this reason that you must seek out people who would be willing to become part of your business and form a team with you.

Anxiety

Indeed, developing anxiety as a result of an overwhelming workload is a very real and crippling feeling that can prove detrimental to not only your work but overall health. However, if you have a team that can handle different obligations, you will feel much happier and healthier when venturing through the tasks of your everyday schedule.

As a young entrepreneur, you might be in high school or college and/or have a job. When you add true entrepreneurship to the mix, you do not have time to waste. It can be absolutely exhausting to wake up every single day and grind at your job, school and business, but when you are able to do this consistently for several years, that is when you will start to reap rewards.

However, if you are trying to accomplish all of this on your own, it is going to end up being a way more difficult task than necessary. This is why taking actions such as networking through social media and conversing with like-minded or interested individuals is crucial. In doing this, you are setting yourself up for success by discussing your vision with potential team members who could end up saving you some time, money and anxiety by accepting certain responsibilities of the business.

Lack of Productivity

Moreover, while having a team saves you some anxiety, it also prevents you from experiencing a lack of productivity. When you are having to work, go to school and be an entrepreneur, you can very easily burn out if you do not give yourself enough time to think and be a human being. With burnout comes carelessness that eventually leads to a lack in the quality of your day to day work and productivity. The last thing you want to become as a young entrepreneur is nonproductive because this will cause your business to dramatically slow down, your following to fade away and clients to search for someone else. If this happens, you will end up losing everything you worked for. Now, in doing this, you end up submitting to society's plans for you, and as many others before you, you will become an entrepreneur that failed because your contentment and lack of productivity caused you to become satisfied with the mediocrity that the system surrounds us with.

Burn Out

The concept of burning out is one that is often discussed in today's society because the subject of mental health has become more prevalent than ever before in popular culture. To define the idea of burning out, it is the equivalent of becoming involuntarily approving of the failure to meet expectations.

Entrepreneurs are very self-driven, determined and ambitious individuals, and while this can lead to a massive amount of success, it can also lead to burnout. When you are extremely determined to constantly accomplish as much as you possibly can with high stress and hardly any breaks for your mind, you are setting yourself up for failure. Having a stellar work ethic is mandatory in order to become a massively successful entrepreneur, but if you are constantly sacrificing your health by skipping meals and missing out on sleep, you will start to feel fatigued, and this will threaten the quality of your work.

As an entrepreneur, you want to ensure that you are giving your followers the highest quality of work possible, but you cannot do this if you are making yourself feel bad by executing your work in an unhealthy manner. Contrary to what some may tell you, the reality is that you do have time, and going to bed at 10:00 pm instead of 1:00 am is not going to be the reason that your business fails.

Very successful and popular entrepreneurs might tell you that college is your enemy, but the reality is that there are true entrepreneurs in college or grade school, and if this is you, realize that there is a time for school and a time for your business. Trying to overlap and overload is going to hurt you on both ends of the spectrum. This can easily be prevented if you understand that you do have time, and the way you feel mentally, physically and spiritually is very much related to the quality of your work.

If you have a team who is being held responsible for certain aspects of your business, this will lighten your load, and you will feel more energized when approaching your role as the entrepreneur. If you are not healthy and motivated, the business and your team is not going to experience near as much success as it should when performing tasks such as interacting with customers, solving problems, brainstorming new ideas, etc.

Now, you cannot expect most or all of your team members to work as hard as you, especially if they do not have ownership. Chances are that you have a sole proprietorship or small partnership when you are first beginning, so the one who is going to work the most regardless at this point is you because you are an owner and founder of the business. On top of that, your team members probably have other obligations that they must fulfill everyday, so you must respect their efforts to accept responsibility and help push your business forward. By all means, do not burn out. Recruit members.

Input

Likewise, another benefit of creating a team is being able to have access to the input of others who come from different circumstances and ways of life. Now, you might have a friend who lives in the same place as you and associates his/herself with the same people, but each of you connect to these people in different ways. Because of that, input from this friend has the potential to become exceptionally valid and can help kick start support for your business.

Moreover, having a team allows you to give your content to those who are on the inside of your business and have the ability to provide you with honest feedback before distributing your products/services to the public. These members can also pitch their own ideas to you, and even if you are not completely on board with their suggestions, you must look at the skill set of the members pitching and the value their ideas could potentially bring to your business by how they impact your followers.

Also, another benefit of having input is specialization. You might have a team member who is great with coding, so placing him/her in charge of your website development might be the best move because this person will know more than the rest when it comes to the process of actually implementing an idea into the website. However, you as the entrepreneur should know what business you are in and what picture you are trying to paint with your brand. You can communicate this with other team members who are specialized. Using the input of your team members will allow you to become satisfying to more people and expand your influence.

Motivating Your Team

In the world of entrepreneurship, self-motivation is a must if you want to produce the best of the best results. Whether it be success, helping others or making money, your motivation can be whatever you want it to be. However, you have to realize that, as the entrepreneur of your business, it is an expectation that you will be the most motivated and passionate person on your team. For this reason, it is important that you are also able to keep your team motivated when completing work related tasks.

First of all, anyone working for your business, whether it be social media focused or an in-person process, should already have a natural motivation to want to contribute to the betterment of the overall business. Nevertheless, you have to keep their thoughts and circumstances in mind as well. They are not the ones who started the business, but they are helping the business reach higher levels of quality and productivity. Think about it this way: if you had a job, you would hopefully want to do well, but chances are that while you do want this, you also want to be able to go home and have your own time. In the same way, your team members are people who want their own time. Understanding this will help them feel happier and more motivated whenever they are completing tasks for your business.

Moreover, as it is important to ensure that you are not being too demanding of your team's personal time, another way to motivate them is by setting an example for them to follow by the way you commit to your job. When a person is being led by someone in a more prestigious position, he/she will find the same standards acceptable that are in adherence with the person in charge. As the leader of your business, you want to make sure that you are holding yourself personally accountable by staying consistently committed to your team, followers and the progression of your business. If your team sees that you are serious and passionate about your job, they will also begin to feel obligated and motivated to hold their own performance accountable.

The way you motivate your team is by making them realize how valuable their roles are, giving them freedom and displaying your passion for the business. In adopting these behaviors, you are setting up a powerful foundation for the longevity of your business and its culture.

Your team plays a crucial role for your business by saving you from headaches and specializing in different aspects of the business so that you can focus on being the entrepreneur. Get to know them know on an individual basis and show them that you care. If you see growth or something positive happen as a result of someone else's efforts, let him/her know. You should always know what results are to be met by each position so that you can show each person that he/she is helping the business progress. If your team knows for a fact that they are contributing to the success of your business, they will take pride in their roles and feel motivated to keep performing at a high level.

Moreover, another way to motivate your team is to give them freedom. If you have a business that is online, let your team members work from bed if they want. You can always video chat to make sure that progress is being made. If you have to meet at a central location every day, maybe you could let them wear their own clothing. Most of the time, work clothes are pretty lame, and we would all feel much happier if we could dress in our street clothes.

This is Generation Z, and it is time to push the envelope on allowing people to be free. Stop worrying about trying to satisfy those before you and suppressing your unique means of expression. We would not be as advanced as we are today if those who put us in this position with their inventions decided not to execute their ideas because someone from an older generation disapproved. For instance, if you have a stock broker, you do not care if he/she wears street clothes. If the value of your portfolio is increasing, you are happy. Push the limits.

Also, another aspect that comes with freedom is creative control. You need to always be open to ideas from your team members whether it is the janitor or an executive. Suggestions or ideas from members, whether you choose to use them or not, are always an asset. If a team member of yours wants to listen to music while working and he/she is not having to talk to customers or associates, let that person listen to music.

Moreover, being at a desk all day can be extremely boring and dead end, so you need to structure your job in a manner that allows employees to move around as well. You want your employees to have fun and feel comfortable because this is what will inspire their creativity. It is your job as the Gen-Z entrepreneur to make your business a place of enjoyment.

We do not have to or need to keep doing things the same way that we have always been taught. Just because you have a financial business does not mean that you have to wear a suit and speak in proper corporate lingo. Entrepreneurship is about innovating and creating new perspectives on reality. If traditionalists disagree with you, then oh well. They are not in your target audience, so inspire team creativity at all costs because that is what will keep your business relevant with the upcoming generations.

Lastly, the most important way to motivate your team is by showing through your actions that you are motivated every single day to do your absolute best. You will not feel like working every single day, but it is your obligation as the entrepreneur to set the tone for your team. When you tune into your business, you set the standard for what is and what is not tolerated. Do you want to allow mediocrity and laziness because someone did not sleep enough the night before? Of course not, so you need to make sure that when you are working, you are the most engaged and seemingly motivated individual on the team.

If your team is able to recognize that you are in tune and happy, it will spread to them. If you cannot show that you are excited and motivated about your business every single day, your team will not either. Set the tone and decide every day that you wake up, you are going to inspire and bring happiness to your team and clients.

How to Start Recruiting

When beginning to build a team, it is wise to take a step back and observe your own personal skill set because this will allow you to analyze your strengths, weaknesses and what does and does not interest you. If there is an aspect of the business that really brings the best performance out of you, then it is wise to stick with that at the beginning.

For instance, let us say that you are starting a social media marketing company, and your most advanced strength is your ability to develop a personal connection with your following by the way you perceive your brand through the designs you develop for the business. If this is the case, you will want to continue creating designs that portray your brand because based off of your followers' reaction to feel personally connected, you are the person for this job.

Nevertheless, even though you might be great at branding, you might not have the strongest set of communication skills. If this is the case, you are going to need someone that can communicate well because people are most likely not going to allow you to manage their social media accounts if you cannot clearly communicate the value you bring to the table. To master a craft is an excellent accomplishment, but if you are only focusing on this aspect, staying in your comfort zone and not letting others in to develop the weaknesses of your business into strengths, you will remain stagnant and eventually close down.

Nowadays, social media has made it to where even the shyest individual can become the most solid recruiter because all this person must do is search for and message potential prospects. There are various platforms to use in order to recruit team members. However, to merely say that social media or even a certain platform is a good route would be too cliché of advice to actually help you recruit members for your business. Here are some more specific ways to go about recruiting team members.

Chat Rooms

Chat rooms that exist on platforms such as Twitter, Facebook, Reddit and website blogs related to your industry are great places to start. The way you go about executing each platform's chat room will be different in certain aspects, but the overall mission is to engage in a conversation with someone who is not merely posting but actually showing knowledge and interest. However, when you are communicating with someone, you need to be sure that you are building rapport by displaying your knowledge through the way you communicate information.

Let us say that you are a stock trader, and your goal is to network with individuals in this industry so that you can potentially find someone to collaborate with and help you research the best chart patterns. You might want to visit Twitter and search for pages related to stocks, the stock market, stock investing, day trading, business, etc. After visiting these pages, you could scroll through posts and read the comments that people are leaving. It is very possible that you might find someone who appears to be knowledgeable on the topic of stock trading. In this case, you could message this person and establish a connection. When you take a step back and decide exactly what you need for your business to be at its strongest, you can take to social media and/or chat rooms to start recruiting.

LinkedIn

If you are looking for a more formal and professional type of platform for recruiting individuals, you could use LinkedIn. This is the most direct social media recruiting source because its entire purpose is to connect employers with potential employees. On this site, people who are looking to get hired in for a job in a specific industry will tailor their profile pages to accordingly by stating their previous experience, education and other credentials that add value to their personal brand. Employers are then able to filter criteria and search for individuals who fit their standards. This platform has become very relevant in the corporate realm and can be very useful if you are wanting to find professionalism.

In the same way, you, as a business owner on LinkedIn, would be able to run a filtered search in order to find potential prospects that would not only be willing but capable of thriving in needed positions. The benefit of LinkedIn is the fact that you can view the experience of those you are speaking with, which helps you determine if these individuals are the right fit for your business. Using LinkedIn for recruitment purposes can serve as a great tool if you are serious about your pursuit and are able to filter your criteria correctly when searching for potential team members to connect with.

Other Social Media

This category consists of your most known platforms such as Twitter, Facebook, Instagram, Snapchat, Reddit, etc. Reddit is the most different because it generally does not welcome business promotion, but you can still spark up a related conversation and build relationships this way. However, on the other platforms, the best way to go about recruiting is by messaging accounts of potential prospects because this does not reveal to the public that your business needs a team.

Typically, hiring out in the open and posting about it is not very influential and can be counterproductive to your growth. People love when they can see a team or an entourage, so being able to sell this image can greatly empower your personal brand as the entrepreneur and that of which your business represents.

Nevertheless, behind the scenes you can search for position fillers, and this will preserve the reputation of your business as well as help you filter out individuals who merely want to be part of your organization for recognition. Messaging others who have shown consistency and knowledge with their own accounts is ideal for recruiting on social media because you are able to validate that these people take their hustle seriously.

Now, when you are hiring someone, you can use a premade message, but it is best to type a personalized one for each person because this lets he/she know that you have really taken the time to study his/her hard work. Put your potential employees' interests before yours when you are going about recruiting because this will show them that you actually care about their success. If you focus on helping your clients and employees with your business, you will be pleased because your business will experience success.

In-Person

This is the classic one that is most praised because it displays confidence and good communication skills. People love a bold entrepreneur who can recruit in person. However, you do not necessarily need to be bold. For instance, you might have friends from mutual organizations who are interested in getting involved. If this is the case, you can test them out by providing them with some objectives to complete and see how this works out over a certain duration of time.

On a bolder note, another thing you can do is approach people at your job or in your classroom with an offer. Nevertheless, you can always print out flyers and head to your local hotspots in order to find potential recruits, but in today's day and age, the most efficient way is most likely going to be through the internet because you can narrow down your search results to specific criteria and bypass extra costs.

CHAPTER ELEVEN:

MANAGING MONEY

CHAPTER ELEVEN

When you think of becoming an entrepreneur, one thing that inevitably comes to mind is money. Money should come to your mind because as stated in the first chapter, whether you are a for profit or non-profit, revenue is going to have to be generated. However, developing revenue is one problem, but managing it can be another when you start to view it with intentions that are contradictory towards the best interest of your business. In order to successfully grow a business, you must know how to successfully manage your money so that it generates value.

Truly, when you are starting out as an entrepreneur, you are most likely going to need access to some amount of funds. If you find that you can start a business at no financial cost and are able to produce revenue, this needs to be reinvested into the business. An example of this would be starting a t-shirt business. Nowadays, you do not need money to start a clothing line. All you need is access to a website to be able to design clothing. After this, you can screenshot the clothing and post it on your website. However, make sure you contact the business of the website you used in order to ensure that it is okay for you to use their property for this reason. Once you do this, you can open a website account such as Shopify and register for a free trial (if still available at the time you read this). This will allow you to kickstart your business on a $0.00 budget and hype it up on social media to your local audience.

However, if you do not have another source of stable and consistent income, you will need to find a job or another means because the last thing you will want is to have to use your profits from the t-shirts to pay for your personal expenses. This could result in your business becoming stagnant and forgotten because you will not have the proper funding to be able to pay for small necessities like a domain or monthly membership fees to the company servicing your site.

Working and/or going to school while being an entrepreneur can be a difficult and exhausting task, but the reality is that you need to be able to support yourself while also producing revenue for your business. Look at every decision as an investment rather than an idea that you hope to see break through. If you do this, you will be more detailed and careful when deciding to create and distribute a product/service to the public.

The reason you want to view your thoughts as an investment is because you want to make money with them. If you only view your idea as something cool that people will purchase because you think it is intriguing, you could become very disappointed and possibly discouraged. Of course, both feelings are part of the journey of entrepreneurship, so you should be prepared for them either way. However, if you were to make an investment with your money into a business, you would want to have realistic reasons as to why you would see a return. In the same way, when you create a product, whether money is spent or not, you want to see a return of more than what you invested.

Moreover, in order to make sure that your money is secure and does not tempt you, you will want to open a bank account solely for your business. This will help because you can connect this account with your means of payment and the money will go straight from your purchasers account to your business account. By doing this, you are setting yourself up for financial success because the funds associated with your business are being held in a separate account that is not being impacted by your personal expenses.

Perception of Money

Earning money as a fresh and new entrepreneur can be one of the most rewarding feelings because it shows that the outside is approving of you and your idea. Nevertheless, if you want to scale up and become a truly established entrepreneur you need to understand that money is a tool for growth.

For example, let us say that you are an author and just published your first book. You and everyone around you is excited, and you feel good about yourself because people are giving you recognition and enjoying your book. After that first check comes in for this book and the hype and sales have slowed down, you realize you have no job. This is a very vulnerable position to be in because you are most likely going to end up using that money for personal use.

However, if you had a job, this would allow you to use the money earned from your book as a means of reinvestment. You could immediately promote your book again and continue to push its popularity forward. In doing this, you would be shifting your perception from that of a consumer to a businessman, and this is what separates an entrepreneur from someone with a mere idea.

An entrepreneur that understands the value of growth is one who understands the value of the perception of money. When you are first starting your business, the wisest decision you could make is to immediately reinvest your profits into your business because this is what is going to help you increase market share and gain credibility.

Goal-Setting

Another way to manage your funds is to set goals for what you hope to accomplish after spending a certain amount. For instance, if you are paying for social media ad promotions, you will want to decide on an amount to spend for a certain duration of time. Make sure that you are carefully defining your target audience when paying for these promotions because if you become lazy, you will end up wasting more money than anticipated since less engagements will occur. Also, make sure that you not only have an intent for a post but that your post aligns with your intent (read that again for understanding if needed). For instance, you may expect to have link clicks to your website, but if you are posting content tailored towards social media profile clicks, you might not produce the exact results you were hoping for, and that is an inefficient means of investing your funds.

It is very possible to make the mistake of spending all your money on adds that get engagements but result in no sales or hardly any true influence. Therefore, it is crucial to know your brand, business and target audience. If you can define these aspects, you will be able to make accurate attempts when running ads or promotions on social media.

Aside from social media, you will also have return on investment (ROI) goals, in more of a physical sense, that you will want to ensure you are satisfying. Let us say that you are someone who regularly replaces phone screens, and most of the time you replace iPhone X screens. If you are wanting to do this on a regular basis, you might consider ordering these screens in advance to speed up the process for your customers. However, if you do not think you can find 100 screens to replace, do not spend your money purchasing 100 iPhone X screens. Instead, you might want to start off ordering 10 because this will be more feasible for you to earn a nice profit. Whether it be directly or indirectly, it is important to always notice if funds for your business are being impacted in any way. Developing cognizance about ROI and how every decision impacts your business' funds is what is going to keep you alive and growing as you continue to provide products/services.

Paying Team Members

If you are a beginning or young entrepreneur, this might seem like a far-fetched idea, but realistically speaking, if you plan on expanding your business and turning it into an LLC or Corporation, you will need to be able to pay your team members. Now, obviously to pay team members you are going to need a source of revenue, and if your business is not yet bringing in the dough, you can either work a job outside of your personal business to be able to pay your employees or hire good salesmen and provide them with necessary commissions. While these are standard ways for a new entrepreneur to pay his/her employees, there are no correct or incorrect methods for doing so. What matters is that, from a financial point of view, each employee hired is a great return on investment.

When you become an entrepreneur, you have many different focuses, but the main underlying one is developing and growing a financially prosperous company that has the ability to bring in consistent streams of revenue. Now, while this might sound obvious, it is important to emphasize that the people you choose to pay for your day to day jobs are viewed as an investment. After all, you are paying them to get the job done in a manner that will add value to the business. If you are paying someone to sell your product, you might want to start off by paying them commission and/or money from your own personal income stream. When you are starting out, these are the types of risks that are necessary to take, and if you are unwilling to invest in yourself, your business or other people, you will not see growth because you will not have the resources or skills to compete with the rest of the market.

Moreover, as time goes on, the hope is that each person you are paying can contribute in a manner that leads to more effective methods of producing profits. If you hire a marketing team, you will want to make sure that they are properly representing the brand of your business and successfully defining markets for your products/services to be sold.

For salesmen, these are the people on the front lines, so when you are paying a salesman, whether it be through commission or another method, you will need to make sure that everything about him/her is properly representing the brand of your business through good customer service, the ability to pitch your products/services, closing deals, etc. Sales is your source of revenue and survival in the world of business and entrepreneurship, and if you do not have good salesmen, you will not be able to keep your company up and running.

Some other considerations could be product development, accounting, law, administrative, etc. Every single one of these departments or employees are an investment that must contribute to the growth in value of your overall business.

If you, as the entrepreneur, decide to pay yourself, you should view your efforts from the same lens and ensure that you are also bringing value to the business. Paying employees who can add value to your business is what will ensure that you are acquiring an adequate return on investment. Hiring the wrong employees could turn out to serve as an expense that outweighs profits and productivity, so it is especially important that you are careful and hiring individuals who are able to show that they are a worthwhile investment for your business.

CHAPTER TWELVE:

SOCIAL MEDIA

CHAPTER TWELVE

Social media has completely taken over the new age of business. If you are a Generation Z entrepreneur wanting to connect your idea to the rest of the world, not only are you in the business of the particular product/service you sell, but you must also be a force in the social media marketing realm. Our generation is constantly on social media apps such as Twitter, Facebook, Instagram, Reddit, Snapchat, etc. If you want to be a true force and build a loyal following, you must be efficiently active on these different platforms and understand how to tailor your marketing for each one.

Note that while we do have access to all platforms (and some may disagree), you do not need to have a profile for all of them. Creating an account for your business on every platform will bring you more exposure, but if you are most familiar with Twitter and your target group consists of Twitter-heavy users, then worrying about a Facebook account is probably not going to be the best move early on. It is important to have exposure, but it is also important to master the art of social media marketing for each platform. You are not going to do this by merely creating an account for each site and posting content. The craft must be mastered for each specific platform, and by specializing in the ones you are most familiar with, you are maximizing the potential for your social media page(s) to generate credibility and revenue.

To gain a deeper insight into what each social media platform offers, let us look at a list of some of the best known.

Facebook

Facebook is the most known and successful social media platform to date. From a functional perspective, Facebook can be characterized as a social networking blog that generally consists of more personal detail sharing than any other major social media platforms. Posts are not limited to a certain amount of characters, so if someone wanted to describe an entire story in a very detailed and intricate manner, then the Facebook platform would allow he/she to do just that.

Facebook is great for business because when running ads and promotions, engagements are generally high if executed at least decently. Facebook is a very good place to begin promoting your business because it has an experienced system for defining a target audience and helping you set your marketing strategies into motion. If you are not sure where to start, you need not worry because Facebook has a team that is more than willing to assist you in setting up your business page and running promotions/ads for specific reasons. Facebook is very welcoming to business and encourages it because revenue is made when businesses pay for advertising. If you want to get your business into the social media realm, Facebook is a quality place to start.

Twitter

Twitter is the epitome of social networking for the new age of the entrepreneur because when trying to target this generation, it provides you with a genuine insight into how people really think on a day to day basis. Someone might have a Twitter and Facebook, but nowadays, many younger adults are starting to use the latter platform less. Twitter posts generally consist of more direct and to the point personal thoughts than other social networking blogs. This platform has become increasingly popular among Generation Z because it is fast, allows us to express ourselves and provides us with a plethora of relative content and up to date humor.

Truly, if Twitter is not the social networking app of the future, it is the biggest step toward that direction. It is huge for upcoming generations because we love our requests to be granted right away, and that is exactly what Twitter does. Yes, other social networks allow for the instant uploading of posts, but Twitter is a microblog, which means that posts are generally shorter than that of other social media networks (Posts are limited to 280 characters). A lot of us do not enjoy reading lengthy pieces of information, and because of this we scroll past long posts immediately. However, with Twitter we can post a lot of one sentence updates throughout the day and get interactions.

Twitter has become somewhat of a live broadcast for our everyday lives. You can guess what someone might be doing at the moment he/she posts. It is also quick because it is not bombarded by spam and advertisements. If you want to know something about someone, the 'About' section is that person's bio, which is posted right below his/her profile picture. These bios are usually a couple of sentences or less, whereas Facebook has an entire section for someone to spill out his/her credentials. Quite frankly, some of us do not care to look at all that information. If you want to make your idea known to this generation, you must be the post that pops up on their feed. They do not care if you have a CPA or if you were born in a barn. They want to see your life through your compact posts. Your relevance window for posting on Twitter runs out very quickly, and what you say at one moment can be forgotten the next, so this is why you must provide concise and constant updates to your page. While Twitter is fast moving, so is the interests of Generation-Z, and that is why it is has such great potential for the future.

Second, another huge benefit of Twitter is the fact that it lets us express ourselves in a way that many of us would not on Facebook or in person. If you want to really get to know someone, you need to view their Twitter profile.

Features such as retweeting (sharing) and liking will tell you so much about a person. Retweeting is Twitter's version of sharing a post, and it fits perfectly with the fast pace that is ingrained in this platform. For instance, let us say that you have an urban clothing line and notice someone showing he/she loves hip-hop music by retweeting and liking posts related to this topic. By seeing this, you can make the correlation that exists between urban wear and hip-hop music. Of course, all types of music artists wear urban clothing, but hip-hop has a huge influence on that aspect of the fashion industry. Because of this, you could make that person a potential target for your clothing sales. In this day and age of individualism and self-expression, Twitter allows us to express ourselves, and if tailored right, your page could be a perfect fit for a defined target audience.

However, while retweets and likes help people express their character, the most concrete expression is a simple post. For instance, maybe you are targeting someone who is having problems and want to help them. If this is the case, you can type key words related to these problems and find those same words in someone else's post. Once you do this, you can follow, retweet, like, DM, etc. in order to direct attention towards your business. Once the attention is directed, you now have the chance to be the answer to this person's problem. However, you must market your page correctly and consistently because if not, it might appear as if you are not serious about your business, and that is not influential to anyone. Using keywords from direct posts can give you a large advantage in getting ahead and growing your following, but you must stay active on a consistent basis in order to serve as a solution and influence for these people.

Lastly, a huge aspect of Twitter is its ability to relate to many teens and young adults on an emotional and humoristic level. The emotions we experience such as happiness, heartbreak, stress and gratitude are very easily expressed on this platform. It often makes it somewhat easier to understand the minds of certain individuals because you can identify through posts what type of person one might portray. As far as humor goes, the Gen-Z source of a good laugh is one that is unique and random. It can be very difficult to understand for some who might be older, but if you plan on using Twitter as a means of social media for your business, you will most definitely want to learn exactly why Gen-Z loves this microblog.

Snapchat

Snapchat is a great platform for allowing your following to visualize your brand and business. If you want to give your followers a more personal insight into your behind the scenes business process, all you have to do is take a photo/video and post it to your story. A story is a photo/video that is posted and can be seen by those of your choosing for up to 24 hours before disappearing or being removed.

When posting on Snapchat, you will want to make sure that your posts consist of visuals and captions that are appealing to the eye. People generally will not want to read an extra-long post, especially if you are a young entrepreneur and have not yet built up a great amount of credibility. Also, if the quality of your pictures is not very good, or if the pictures made to promote your business do not look very professional, this could potentially be a shot to the reputation of your brand and business.

Snapchat is an app that has the potential to become a very powerful tool for you when it comes to building your brand and marketing your business. If you can use it in a manner that is influential to your specific audience, you will find that it will serve as a very good compliment to the success of your business. In the world of entrepreneurship, influence is a major component when it comes to selling your audience on your authenticity and vision.

Instagram

Instagram is similar to Snapchat because it is all about pictures, but it is also like Facebook and Twitter because it allows for longer captions and actual profile pages that can be viewed. When managing an Instagram account for your business, you want to make sure that you develop a recurring theme. In doing this, newcomers viewing your page will be able to tell what your business does right away and decide if they are interested. However, if you are always changing your content in drastic ways, and none of your posts are correlated, it might be very difficult for you to gain traction in any niche market that exists on Instagram.

The main powerplay for Instagram is exceptional pictures and quality videos. Instagram is a powerhouse for many businesses within the retail space because it allows them to provide powerful visuals of certain products. Many high end clothing companies such as Supreme, Off White, Alexander Wang and others are constantly posting to Instagram in order to market their products because they realize that a substantial portion of their target audience exists on this platform.

Moreover, videos are also a quality product that Instagram offers, and many entrepreneurs such as Gary

Vaynerchuk and Grant Cardone use them as a tool to express themselves and build up their personal brand. Instagram videos have the power to be a major influence on your following if done in a manner that is not dull to their eyes. This is why Gary Vaynerchuk has added features such as captions, logos and even signature sounds that you can become familiar with and know that it is indeed him who is about to be played through your phone.

Instagram is a heavily used app among Generation Z, and with many of our influencers presenting their products and remaining relevant with us on this app, it seems as though it will continue to be a major force for many years to come. If you are an entrepreneur and want to show your products to the world, Instagram is arguably the best platform you could use.

Reddit

Reddit is different from other social media platforms because rather than encouraging business promotion, it discourages it. This site serves as a forum for different communities who are focused on discussing specific topics. For example, one who is interested in gaming can easily type in, "gaming" and find related communities that will allow him/her to subscribe and communicate on gaming topics with other subscribers of this community. The downfall of Reddit is the fact that, when it comes to business, it is not going to benefit you as much in the short run because it does its best to shut out promotions. You will often find that you have been banned from a community after posting a link to your site or a certain product/service you are selling.

Nevertheless, Reddit can be very useful in the long run if you are willing to truly get involved with certain communities and legitimately discuss topics without trying to directly sell your business. As time progresses, you will start to become more familiar with your community and learn what exactly people do and do not want to hear. At the same time you are doing this, you can name your profile the same as your business, and this could potentially intrigue some individuals enough to explore further into what you are all about. However, while Reddit is good in the long run, it should not be your primary source of engaging in business on social media.

Analytics Apps

In order to run a successful social media page, you need to have apps that record analytics for your profile. These apps come with a variety of statistical data that can be used to help you tailor your page and posts in a way that will attract your target audience. For instance, let us say that you just started a profile on Instagram and followed 2,000 people related to your industry but realized not all followed back. There are apps that will allow you to unfollow these accounts. You can also type in keywords and save them in a page that will direct you to accounts related to these words.

On the more post related side, you can see which posts had the most views and interactions instead of just seeing the likes. Comments per post, likes per posts, follows per posts, etc. are other statistics that can be seen and used in a beneficial manner. The only way this could fail you is if you fail yourself by not staying patient, consistent and dedicated to mastering the demographics of your target audience. Nowadays, people will sell you that it takes just a few months to start earning x amount of dollars per month with your business, but if it were so simple that it only took a few months to develop an influential business and brand that accumulated thousands of dollars worth of sales, everyone would quit their day job and have their own online business.

Distraction

While social media can be an absolute gold mine for every single entrepreneur, it can also serve as a distraction if used impulsively and too frequently. As entrepreneurs, we get a high from accomplishment and perfecting our business, but if you are one that is constantly posting nonsense because you want to gain personal recognition, you are selling yourself and your business short in a variety of ways. Content for social media should be posted on a regular basis, but if it is not done in a manner that adds appreciating value to your brand, then it should not be uploaded.

Indeed, as an entrepreneur, you want to be heard, and you want your idea to be known, but there is a right way and wrong way specific to every audience. It is up to you to find the right balance of this because the last thing you want for yourself is to be someone who is posting so many videos that you are just carelessly speaking cliché nonsense that is either unrelated or damaging to your business. It is important to always stay focused on your work because that is your product at the end of the day. Social media is important, but if you have no work to offer, you do not have any value.

Use social media as a tool to add value to your business rather than a place where you can stroke your ego, and you will have long-term success. A true entrepreneur always asks what his/her business can do for others rather than what it can do for his/herself. If you can answer this question, you will be able to stay focused and make wise decisions when posting to your social media profile(s).

CHAPTER THIRTEEN:

EMOTIONAL INTELLIGENCE

CHAPTER THIRTEEN

It is all too easy, as an entrepreneur, to make the mistake of mismatching energy levels with your team members and audience. Considering the fact that this is your business vision being put to work, you are going to be the most passionate and ambitious about its success. However, while any entrepreneur should be the most excited about his/her business idea, the team and following that he/she communicates with might not feel that same amount of enthusiasm. Because of this, it is important to make decisions that are emotionally intelligent and in sync with the feelings of those associated with you.

The ability to understand how your audience is feeling is essential to your reputation and capability as an influence. Emotional intelligence is one of the most overlooked aspects of not just entrepreneurship but life in general. Some are not sure what this means because it is a topic that is typically not discussed to the necessary extent. Nevertheless, having emotional intelligence is key to becoming an influential communicator, and without influential communication, entrepreneurship is impossible because you will not be able to sell people on your ideas.

What is Emotional Intelligence?

Emotional intelligence is the ability to gauge how an individual is feeling at a certain moment for the purpose of being able to match that energy. For example, not everyone is a morning person, so if you are one who is, you might not want to approach those who are not with an incredibly energetic attitude. This could irritate and cause them try to avoid you because you might come off as annoying. It is difficult to be a leader and influence others if you annoy or upset them in some way. To be emotionally intelligent means to be able to recognize and match the energy that someone is portraying through their verbal and nonverbal communication.

To gain a clearer understanding, think about the main influencers in your friend group. They may or may not be the most talkative ones, but their ability to empathize and match everyone's energy is what helps these friends connect in the most effective and influential manner. People who portray an overkill of a certain emotion tend to get socially shunned because everyone is not constantly feeling one way, and it can be very damaging to your ability to influence if you are always amplifying one type of emotion or energy.

If you are posting on social media, you want to be very careful with how you are portraying yourself because if you are too egotistical or emotional, this could cause people to lose interest in you or your business. Always keep a level of maturity when you are presenting your ideas because without this, it might not seem that you are being realistic about your business. You are in business to influence and help others, but without profits a business cannot survive long enough to be able to perform these tasks. Considering that influence leads to profits, if emotional intelligence is absent on social media, people could potentially decide to not visit your profile page or website, and this will decrease your sales.

How to Instill Emotional Intelligence

The first step to becoming emotionally intelligent is having the ability to read someone. In order to do this, you must learn to take what people give you. It is very possible that someone around you is going through the worst possible circumstances, but if they are portraying a happy and positive attitude when working, it is either because they feel they cannot communicate with you about their problems, or they feel that work is their happy place. We are going to use "place" as a general term because business relationships can solely exist over the internet or with a group of team members at different locations.

Nevertheless, empathizing with your team is key to emotional intelligence because even if someone is lying to you about how they feel, you at least showed that you cared about that person's well-being by asking how he/she felt. When your team knows that you value and care about them, that is when the best work will be produced. You do not make and/or influence friends by offsetting your emotional gauges. When energies are matched, people connect.

Branding is another crucial aspect of your business, and in order to add influence and power to your brand, you must execute it in an emotionally intelligent manner. Think about how you would feel towards your celebrity influences if they were to raid their social media with constant egotistical statements. Some might find this appealing, but if it is frequent and you see this every time you get on Twitter, it has the potential to eventually become annoying.

This is exactly what you do not want for your business as an up and coming entrepreneur. A perfect example of this would be Kanye West ranting on Twitter about Drake being at fault and doing wrong to him. While this got much attention, it did not serve well for the brand of Kanye. If anyone was going to get away with this, it was going to be an A-list celebrity like Kanye. However, if you are new to the game, the last thing you want to do is act in a way that is emotionally ignorant and mismatched with the energy of your followers.

In order to have success as an entrepreneur, you must act in an emotionally intelligent manner because this is what is going to allow you to influence individuals. Without the ability influence, you are not going to be able to grow an audience or a team. In a way, you must make friends with your following. To elaborate, think about how you make friends and influence those in your circle. You should have the same mentality when building a relationship with your following because having that awareness will allow you to act in an emotionally intelligent manner no matter what you are doing.

CHAPTER FOURTEEN:

LEADERSHIP

CHAPTER FOURTEEN

If you have a job or ever had to work with people in a group setting, you might have noticed who it was that took initiative and made the purpose of the team easier to understand. These people were the leaders of the team because they brought the accountability out of you that made you want to participate and add value to the project your group was assigned. In the same way, an entrepreneur must be a leader to the rest of his/her team in order to bring out each member's best performance.

Leadership is not as easy and concrete to define as the way some make it seem. It is a highly generalized topic, and it is rare that you see it properly discussed. You do not have to be an extrovert who says hello to everyone in order to be a leader. You can be an introvert and lead by example. To be a leader does not mean you are in a position of power. It means that you are able to bring out the best in those around you. You are not just making sure that objectives are being met, but you are actively involving yourself with your peers and trying to make them better each day.

Not A Manager

To understand true leadership, let us first explore what is confused with leadership but is not actually equal; managing. Using a similar example to the one discussed earlier, in school or at your job, you had group work or discussions, and during these sessions, you had individuals who were assigned as "leaders." However, some of these people were probably not leaders but instead managers because rather than trying to bring the best out in you, these "leaders" of your groups only made sure that the expectations of an overseer was met. In the same way, if you are an entrepreneur and only setting goals to be met, that does not make you the leader. As a matter of fact, you can be the entrepreneur, and a different team member might be the leader of your business. Managing is not leading, and you should constantly be developing your leadership skills in order to instill intrinsic value and pride in your team.

The Leader Within You

If you want to lead your team, you must find what it is about you that is most valuable when it comes to interacting with people because that is what you are going to use to lead. Some people are extroverts and love to interact and talk with others, so that is most likely where they are best at leading. However, you can lead just by staying consistent with your work and showing a happy face every day because that impacts your team and helps bring out the best in them. Leadership is not about you. It is about those around you. When you are a leader, you are thinking of ways to use yourself in order to bring out the best in your peers.

Successful entrepreneurs know how to lead and are aware that there are countless ways to go about doing so. For instance, you might be a polarizing and influential person with a great aura when you walk into the room, and that in itself will energize and inspire people to want to be their best. There is no right or wrong way to lead. Either you are or are not bringing out the best in those around you.

How to Become A Leader

As stated earlier, being a leader is about those around you. If you want to be able to bring the best out in people, you need to know how each individual thinks and communicates. Not everyone wants to be placed on a pedestal for their accomplishments. For a more quiet-natured type of person, maybe just a pat on the back or friendly text will do. You have to know how individuals operate emotionally and logically because this will empower your ability to influence them in a way that brings out their best performance.

You become a leader when you decide to set the gold standard for not only professional performance but also character performance. A leader does not treat his/her team in a disrespectful manner when something goes wrong. Instead, he/she comforts them and asks what can be done to assure that the mistake does not happen twice. Having exceptional character is crucial to leadership because if you, as the entrepreneur, set a high standard, your team will follow. However, if you set a low standard of character, your team will follow this as well, but this will upset customers and cause your business to quickly collapse. A leader always sets the tone and standards for his/her associates, and in doing so, is able to serve as an influence that raises the overall performance and happiness of the team.

Ethics

Before accomplishing anything in entrepreneurship or business, a wise individual will assure his/her ethics. Without ethics, absolutely nothing about your business has true value. Ethics is not merely about telling the truth, but it is also about intent. Are you making decisions at the expense of others in order to benefit yourself? If so, greed can only take a business so far. When an individual on a team is greedy, he/she acts in a way that is dissatisfying to the best interest of everyone else. Because of this, stakeholders start to become unimpressed with this business for the simple fact that it merely serves to satisfy the ego of the entrepreneur instead of the problems of the customers.

The best interest of your customers and team must always come first when providing products/services. This will keep a recurring satisfaction among all stakeholders, which means that there will be a higher chance of producing a steady stream of revenue. To have a truly successful start to end as a business, you must make ethics the primary focus.

CHAPTER FIFTEEN:

BUSINESS TYPES

CHAPTER FIFTEEN

It can be a boring and seemingly daunting task, but as they say, the boring things matter most. That is why having a necessary understanding of how laws and the IRS relate to your business is crucial to your establishment and longevity.

The last thing you will want as a young or new entrepreneur is to be held personally liable for a mistake that could have been easily avoided. Understanding how laws relate to different types of ownership and your specific industry will help you have a much smoother sailing ride than if you do not take the time to learn them.

Types of Ownership

Sole-Proprietorship

The sole-proprietorship is the most basic form of business, and it is very simple to establish. As a sole proprietor, you are your business. All of the rewards and losses are under your responsibility, and you are personally liable for all decisions made.

From a banking and tax point of view, a sole proprietorship does not require you to have any extra accounts or tax filings, which makes it simple for someone who is new to starting a business. When establishing this form of business, you can use a personal checking account under your name in order to deposit the funds of business transactions. You will be responsible for claiming taxes on your personal income tax return however, so it is important that you keep records of every sale made.

Also, while it is recommended that you obtain an employer identification number (EIN), most sole proprietors can instead use their social security number (SSN). This is how the IRS will hold you responsible for paying taxes.

For new and/or young entrepreneurs looking to get started with their business, a sole proprietorship is a great and simple route to begin with because it is easy to start up and does not require too many details to get started.

Partnership

A partnership is defined as a business that is owned by two or more individuals that come together to make a profit. Partners share in the profits and operations of the business based on the duties and percentage of ownership and that has been agreed upon.

Nevertheless, each owner is "jointly and severally liable" for debts and damages.

In a partnership, you must be careful when choosing who to share the business profits and responsibilities with because by law, if someone is entitled to a certain percentage of profits, and duties are not clearly defined, you could end up having to compromise your compensation with someone who is not contributing an adequate amount of work to the progression of the business.

As far as paying taxes goes, each partner is taxed based off of his/her own percentage of profits. The partnership itself cannot be taxed. Again, this is another way to know that you can be held personally liable for debts and damages created by the business.

Limited Liability Company (LLC)

If you are worried about personal liability issues, you might want to consider becoming a limited liability company (LLC) because you and the business will be judged as two different entities. The IRS will treat an LLC as a sole proprietorship or partnership based on the number of members involved. However, in regard to taxes, an LLC is taxed as a partnership, which means that each member is personally taxed based off of his/her profits made from the business. However, you can also elect to be taxed as a corporation. The largest benefit of an LLC is the fact that it protects members from being held personally liable for debts and damages.

Another important point to know about LLCs is the role of the operating agreement. An operating agreement discusses the terms and allocation of financial obligations among members. This document also states the structure of governing power and decision making within the business, and it serves as a binding agreement that must be followed once signed by all members. However, an operating agreement is not a requirement, and if one is not drafted, the LLC must operate by the rules of its state government.

Corporation

A corporation is the most complex form of business because it has many different contributors with access to profits and differing levels of liability. The first thing to understand about a corporation is that it is taxed as a separate entity from the people employed by it. A corporation is owned by shareholders who have rights to shares of stock within the business. The business can either be public or private. If it is public, this means the business is listed on a public exchange and individuals have the right to purchase shares of stock from this business as they please.

If the business is private however, the public does not have the right to purchase shares of stock, but instead members of the business are given shares in accordance with the agreement decided upon by the board of directors. Shareholders have a right to vote on who is appointed to the board of directors. The board of directors oversees management activities and makes decisions in regard to compensation and executive appointments. They must keep the best interest of the shareholders at the forefront of their decisions because they are ambassadors for them and must try their best to ensure that profits are being produced.

CHAPTER SIXTEEN:

MEETINGS

CHAPTER SIXTEEN

A business planning to grow and improve in all of its specific departments must have meetings in order to maintain the quality of the time and energy being invested into the vision. When you are starting out, the importance of having meetings can be easily overlooked, but until you begin to do this, you will not grow at your best potential rate. Meetings are a necessity if you want to succeed as a business because they allow your team to communicate valuable information and suggestions that serve the purpose of allowing your business to grow in a variety of ways while scaling up.

Connection

Having chemistry with your team is one of the most valuable assets to possess because it means that everyone understands each other as not only co-workers but human beings who have knowledge and emotion. The more meetings you have, the more chemistry your team will be able to build because they will start to understand one another better.

You can host a livestream at any desired time with another member who might be across the globe. Doing this allows you to familiarize yourself with the personality and roles of each individual working with you. As the entrepreneur, you need to take the initiative to get everyone on the same page and talking with each other because this is what will keep the team in sync with the overall mission of the business.

Not having meetings could result in a lack of motivation for members, which could eventually result in a lack of performance. If you want to have a good connection with your team and an understanding of their strengths and weaknesses, you must have productive and purposeful meetings.

Live Streaming

Live streaming has the potential to be the most useful type of meeting for you and your team if it is being efficiently executed. When you live stream, you are working on your business with other members who are not in the same location as you but are able to see you and communicate through a computer or smartphone screen. This is just like working side by side, and you will have some quiet moments, but that is how it is supposed to be. It is not a scheduled meeting. You are working together, building chemistry and sharing ideas. So much can be learned through live streaming because you are able to set an example for your employees by the way you work and communicate on a minute by minute basis.

As a young entrepreneur, if you are only texting your team members, you cannot communicate as well and instill an adequate level of accountability in them. If you are constructing a schedule or working on your website, you will want to have a livestream with your team because this will allow you to work together in real time, whereas if you are texting, you cannot properly communicate what should and should not be changed about the website. This could result in you doing all the work and your team members waiting for your approval through a text to make any moves at all. The amount of chemistry that can be built with live streams are unmatchable, and the productivity level has the potential to be at its highest if executed properly.

Another benefit of hosting live streams is the fact that your team gets to see how serious you are about your business, which will instill accountability in them and strengthen their commitment to the overall vision. You must take advantage of this time and lead by example. For instance, if you start to find yourself feeling bored during a stream, do not communicate that you are bored. That energy will spread to your team and can lead to a lack of true commitment on any given day. Instead, what you need to do is show that you are focused and engaged. It is important to get to business and complete tasks, but you also want to encourage your members to have fun and enjoy life. If no one is happy when they are working, there is no reason at all to keep working, especially if everyone has a full-time job and your business is currently a side hustle. However, it is your job as the entrepreneur to lead by example and efficiently instill accountability in your team members through live streams.

Scheduled Meetings

While live streams are more informal and similar to working side by side, scheduled meetings serve the purpose of pausing for a moment in order to observe the position of the team and improve on any mishaps that might be taking place. This will ensure that the business is on track to meet its objectives. Scheduled meetings are more formal in the information that is being distributed because they typically involve viewing the business from a larger perspective as opposed to the day to day streaming where you are dealing with every little problem and concept that you encounter.

Before you schedule meetings, you need to have an agenda for what you are going to discuss because this will ensure that you do not miss any important points. This type of meeting is a critical tool to use in order to ensure your team is on the same page and focused on expectations for the future.

CHAPTER SEVENTEEN:

UNIQUENESS IS GENIUS

CHAPTER SEVENTEEN

We often see legends such as Dr. Dre, Jay-Z, Kanye West, Michael Jackson, Quentin Tarantino, etc. classified as geniuses. Any time these names are said, there is a respected and unique distinction that can instantly be made with each of them. Every successful entrepreneur is a genius in his/her own way because that person was able to see an opportunity and capitalize on it in a profitable and influential manner.

Truly, uniqueness is genius. Yes, these individuals have had a great amount of success that gives them an edge of respect, but the truth is that these people were geniuses way before any of the accolades. What makes them special is instead of loving what they do, they do what they love.

When you wake up every single day, what do you do that makes you happy, or what do you wish you could do? We often hear people tell us to do what we love, and that is completely real. However, once we start doing what we love, we sometimes lose confidence in ourselves because we are not taken seriously right away. You must look at it this way: when Kanye West was young and unknown, he was in his room 12 plus hours per day mastering his craft, and nobody was there to give him a pat on the back. When you are genuinely happy doing something, that is your escape, and you do not need validation (at least not immediately) because that alone brings you enjoyment.

When you genuinely enjoy something, you bring natural uniqueness to it. It becomes an art form, and that is the uniqueness your brand needs in order to become influential. It is too easy to get discouraged because maybe a particular post on social media did not get enough interactions. Yes, interactions and social media engagements are important, but you cannot concentrate your value solely on that. Saying to not focus on it means that maybe you should post a piece of your craft online and delete your social media app. This is totally a possibility, and some would argue that you should keep social media in order to interact with others about your post. However, if you just post and wait a few hours or days, you can easily go back to your post and see how it was received.

Genius is not something that is always immediately appreciated, and some people might find you weird because you probably act differently than most of the crowd. That is not to fear however, as you should realize that genius is often misunderstood. It is not common for someone to be his/her complete self to the rest of the world, and when that happens, people around you might not know how to exactly perceive it at first. Do not act discouraged. Be a boss, have confidence in your uniqueness and keep giving content to the world.

Jacob M. Melendez

VICTORY LAP

Platinum Entrepreneur

Photo taken by: Nancy Le

This section is called, “Victory Lap” not because it has to do with entrepreneurship, but because it has to do with life. I would like to take this time to thank everyone that has helped me up to this point and provided me with the strength and confidence to be able to fully express myself and pursue my ambitions. This is not just a book, and it is not just a dream or a life. It is the manifestation of a true vision for a platinum reality. This vision is larger than myself, and it is larger than you, the reader.

Celebrate yourself and do exactly what you want. It is going to be difficult, and it might not happen after all, but you get one life in human history, and you have to be willing to try. We spend so much time grinding and trying to acquire the most prestigious job, position, paycheck, etc. and we forget that life is a gift. If you are happy and whole with what you are currently doing, that is your art, and you should take pride in that.

When I was a sophomore in high school, all I wanted to do was become the best. I dreamed of it, and I wanted nothing less that that. I did not sell myself short, but I instead did what I needed to do in order to get where I am today. I am now the founder of Elevate (a company that aims to educate younger generations on business and finance) and Excite Publishing.

Platinum Entrepreneur

Jacob M. Melendez

ABOUT THE AUTHOR

Jacob M. Melendez is an investor and entrepreneur who serves as the Founder/Owner of *Elevate* and *Excite Publishing*. He is also a manager of the cryptocurrency startup project, *KuboCoin*.

The idea of how a business is developed from a person's mind and converted into a successful money making machine has intrigued Jacob from adolescence. Through his experience of starting *Elevate*, which is a business that aims to educate the youth on business and finance, Jacob has been able to gain rare insight that has provided him with a solid knowledge base on not only what it takes to become successful in this day and age in business, but also the struggles that young and/or new entrepreneurs face.

Jacob M. Melendez

Photo taken by: Nancy Le

Platinum Entrepreneur

BIBLIOGRAPHY

Goel, Naval. "The 7 Stages of Entrepreneurship." *Entrepreneur*, 27 Apr. 2017, www.entrepreneur.com/article/293463.

Philbeck, Thomas, and Kaj Työppönen. "What Is Hypergrowth, and What Can We Learn from It?" *World Economic Forum*, 2016, www.weforum.org/agenda/2016/04/what-is-hypergrowth why-does-it-matter/.

Council, Young Entrepreneur. "Five Tips For Managing Hyper-Growth That Every Startup Needs." *Forbes*, Forbes Magazine, 7 Dec. 2017, www.forbes.com/sites/theyec/2017/12/07/five-tips-for-managing hyper-growth-that-every-startup-needs/#77c9b63c3d20.

LII Staff. "Partnership." *Legal Information Institute*, Legal Information Institute, 20 Nov. 2018,

"Limited Liability Company LLC | Internal Revenue Service." *Limited Liability Company LLC | Internal Revenue Service*, www.irs.gov/businesses/small-businesses-self-employed/limited-liability-company-llc.

Beesley , Caron. "6 Things You Need to Know About Your Tax Responsibilities as an LLC." *Small Business Administration*, 2012, www.sba.gov/blogs/6-things-you-need-know-about-your-tax-responsibilities-llc.

Kenton, Will. "LLC Operating Agreement." *Investopedia*, Investopedia, 12 Mar. 2019, www.investopedia.com/terms/l/llc-operating-agreement.asp.

www.ingramcontent.com/pod-product-compliance
Lightning Source LLC
Chambersburg PA
CBHW021418210526
45463CB00001B/439

* 9 7 8 1 7 9 5 1 6 5 7 9 2 *